*D*RIVEN

John Skoyles

MADHAT PRESS
ASHEVILLE, NORTH CAROLINA

MadHat Press
MadHat Incorporated
PO Box 8364, Asheville, NC 28814

The Library of Congress has assigned
this edition a Control Number of
2018956371

ISBN 978-1-941196-78-6 (paperback)

Cover art by Paul Resika: *Starry Night,* 1947, oil on canvas, 40"x45.5"
Courtesy Berta Walker Gallery, Provincetown, MA

Cover design by Marc Vincenz
Book design by MadHat Press

www.madhat-press.com

First Printing

Advance Praise for *Driven*

Driven is a tender account of matters sorting themselves in the autumn of life. It inspires an awakening, which is to live well, to pay attention to every fraught atom of sorrow and joy, and to be grateful. Skoyles shows us the intricate way *moment meets memory,* as his meditations on his life reveal a sensibility that is all too rare.

—AFAA M. WEAVER, author of *The Government of Nature* and *Spirit Boxing*

John Skoyles' *Driven* is a series of evocative miniatures that explore the past, memory, and how we reconcile our ambition—our intimate drives and what drives us. Skoyles is also well aware of what we can't control, how we are not always in control, how we are sometimes passengers driven by others. These stories are gorgeously rendered lyrics, mature in their observations, and breathtakingly sublime in their imagery. Skoyles writes prose odes to loss, impermanence, to saying goodbye, affirming a life well-lived, a life filled with friendship and love.

—DENISE DUHAMEL, author of *Blowout* and *Ka-Ching!*

In *Manhood: A Journey from Childhood into the Fierce Order of Virility,* Michel Leiris writes, "I am imbued with the notion that a Muse is necessarily a dead woman, inaccessible or absent; that the poetic structure—like the canon, which is only a hole surrounded by steel—can be based only on what one does not have; and that ultimately one can write only to fill a void or at the least to situate, in relation to the most lucid part of ourselves, the place where this incommensurable abyss yawns within us." It's difficult to think of a more exact précis of John Skoyles' extraordinary new book, *Driven,* which is an obsessive, eloquent, bittersweet, tragicomic, and utterly persuasive meditation on the relationship between loss (the marker of human existence) and imagination (the marker of art). Leiris's book is great; so is Skoyles'.

—DAVID SHIELDS, author of *Reality Hunger* and *The Trouble with Men: Reflections on Sex, Love, Marriage, Porn, and Power.*

for Judith Grossman

Other Books by John Skoyles

POETRY

A Little Faith
Permanent Change
Definition of the Soul
The Situation
Suddenly It's Evening: Selected Poems
Inside Job

PROSE

Generous Strangers
Secret Frequencies: A New York Education
A Moveable Famine: A Life in Poetry
The Nut File

Table of Contents

John Skoyles

Preface

This is a story of lost love. And lost time. And the losses everyone bears. The loss of father and mother. Sometimes of children. Always of lovers. Often of self. Losses everyone fears. Life which begins to end as soon as it begins. This living and dying at once along a stretch of years that the more they go forward, the more we look back, making up a shawl of memories comprised of micro-memories. And toward the end, even the past shrinks, leaving us alone with a demanding present and a short future. So this is also a story of lost life. *Yet for all your pains, try a little laughter,* Rabelais said. If life is a symphony of disappointments, it is a symphony nevertheless. If a life is crisscrossed with renunciations, it is still a life. My father's last words were *If I knew then what I know now ...* What did he mean? Was he referring to a singular event, or a major path he should have taken? Do we ever finish knowing? What is the distance between then and now?

I can't sleep. There is a woman stuck between my eyelids. I would tell her to get out if I could. But there is a woman stuck in my throat.
        —*Eduardo Galeano*

"It is I and it is not I," she said. "You shall find me again and you shall lose me."
        —*Marcel Schwob*

To the tortoise, all ages are one; all wounds, contemporary.
        —*Eugenio Montale*

I dreamt the past was never past redeeming.
        —*Richard Wilbur*

The dead must stay in their graves. That's what graves are for.
        —*Robert Penn Warren*

It is undone business / I speak of, this morning, / with the sea / stretching out / from my feet.
        —*Charles Olson*

And so they are ever returning to us, the dead.
        —*W. G. Sebald*

A Wild, Rank Place

"A man may stand there and put all America behind him," the National Park Service's website quotes Thoreau's words describing Cape Cod. He also called it, "a wild, rank place," but that's not the kind of welcome to set before tourists. It's six o'clock on a spring morning, and I am getting ready to drive the one hundred miles from my house in Truro, the smallest town on the Cape, to Boston. Like everyone with a long commute, I leave parts of myself along the way. By the time I arrive at Emerson College where I work, I have been pecked by a gauntlet of painful memories, ravaged ambitions, and thwarted desires. I fight traffic, gesturing to drivers both rapacious and slow. I yell at those who stick to one lane and those who cut in and out. When I enter the city, I curse the pedestrians and when I walk from where I park my car, I curse the vehicles.

Yet today will be different—today I make the last trip of the year. Today is different from other days when I gauge the time it takes to reach the fast-food stops where I eat, drink, and relieve myself before arriving at my destination. Today I dedicate myself to appreciating each moment of the trip as if it is a gift and not a trial, although my father's words still haunt me. What did he regret? One wrong turn, or an error-filled map? *Now* for me means it's time to dress in the dawn and get on the road. Along the way, a world of dreams, a world of *then*: an ex-girlfriend; the dump dance; Lupo's Heartbreak Hotel; Helen Keller's bathing suit; the dive bar, Aces High; my mother's puns and my father's advice; a sick goose and a taste of infinity.

Today I will forget Raymond Roussel's belief that "the best place to travel is in your own room," and savor Camilo José Cela's slogan, "Everything that comes along is always the best thing that could happen." In an hour or so, I will drive as if the lanes of the Southeast Expressway are green pastures, as if I am going of my own free will.

SOLITARY

I brew a single-serve coffee and face the paintings on my walls, paintings I love but, over time, I've come to see each as a prison cell, a small square of solitary confinement in which the artist has paced. This is because I know the painters well, many of them celebrated, all of them friends, each with a singular neurosis, trapped behind these rectangles as if behind bars, trying to scratch through the back of the canvas and puncture the surface. I cannot look at the paintings without seeing divorce, death, and madness clanging their metal cups against the wooden braces stretched across every frame. Not one is even-keeled. Each has been through a trauma, and some are ongoing. When the phone rings, it is often an artist's voice clenched by betrayal, alcohol, disease, or debt.

I stop at another unhappy portrait: a mirror. I do this to smooth what little hair I have down from the one spiraling peak I woke with, not a man-bun or top-knot, but a few refugee strands like those from a game of pin-the-tail-on-the-donkey. As more hair is lost, my ears spring more widely from my head, and I recall my mother proudly saying I had inherited her family's "Bertolotti ears," which she claimed could receive as well as broadcast thoughts.

The Victorian brass lamp from the Plaza Hotel on Central Park, its tin shade olive green, provides fine light. When I was sixteen, my Aunt Mae asked me to meet her in the lobby; the management was updating its decor and selling old furnishings and utensils. In the grand ballroom, the hoi polloi examined silverware and stemware as well as couches, arm chairs, and vases. I carried this lamp, a clock radio, and two crystal ashtrays back to Mae's apartment in Queens where she lived alone all her life. When she died, I inherited this lamp, which had illuminated the pages and paths of so many strangers, and which reminds me of my solitary aunt who spent her evenings reading Evelyn Waugh and Edna Ferber. Mae once quoted the latter to me, saying, "Being an old maid is a great deal like death by drowning—a really delightful sensation when you cease struggling."

Good morning, Aunt Mae, never married and long dead. I regret you had to struggle at all.

A Lucky Man

I drink the coffee in my own cell, at a small table near Paul Resika's oil of a ship's prow crossing a blue horizon toward an orange moon. In the *New York Times,* Hilton Kramer called Resika, "a master of color with a loaded brush." Paul stands apart from the others: always bright and resilient, perhaps the secret of his eighty-nine years. He is married to a beautiful woman, Blair, and his beautiful daughters are devoted to his work. Once I went to lunch with him at the Olde Reliable Fish House, where we were served by an angelic blonde college student. Paul said to her, "We're both close to heaven. You through beauty, me through age." Very charming. But at the end of the meal, when he requested a cup of coffee with a scoop of vanilla ice cream in it, she declined. It wasn't on the menu. Even her refusal contained a piercing shard of beauty, though with an aftertaste of despair.

Resika is a lucky man. When Parsons School of Design asked him to start an MFA program, he accepted on his own terms: only artists would lecture (no critics), he would attend no meetings, and everyone enrolled would receive financial aid. I met one of his former students, now a well-known painter still devoted to his teacher. He said Resika was a brilliant instructor, and he laughed as he recalled seeking Resika's help twice. When he was stuck on a painting, he raised his hand and Resika walked over, stood by his easel, and said, "Spit on your palette! Spit on it!" The student spat, and though saliva failed to solve the dilemma, he said he learned to be ruthless in revision. The second time Resika came to his canvas, he looked at it, frowned, and said, "*Coraggio!* That's what the Italians say, *Have courage!*" At the last class, Resika gave a little lecture, saying that in every relationship there is a driver and a passenger, and the students had to decide which they will be, not only in romance but in the practice of art. Then he presented each young painter with a copy of Delacroix's *Journal.*

One day I called Paul to tell him a pastel of his was on eBay, a shapely backside of a reclining nude purported to be that of Mariette Hartley, the TV personality. He repeated this information aloud for the benefit of his household, and I heard a buzz of conversation in the background.

"Hold on, Skoyles," he said. "What? What? Oh, okay," he said to someone in the room. "Skoyles," he continued, "my daughters are here. They know about it, they've seen it. They say it's a drawing of Blair. It's my drawing of Blair up for auction."

Paul has brought the images of many beautiful women to his canvasses. As I said, Resika is a lucky man

Today I will try to channel some of his joie de vivre, but as I look out the window it begins to rain, even as the sun is shining, and the water in the gutter drips toward the earth with the sound of the second hand of a clock.

EPITAPH

My wife is asleep upstairs, an arrangement we've had since we moved here twenty-four years ago, to our first two-story house. At that time, our toddler son, Harry, afraid to be alone on the ground floor, ran to us every night, so I moved next to him, to this bedroom/study where I spend a lot of time inventing epitaphs for my wife's gravestone— yes, because if I were alone, I could sell the house, quit my job, move to a studio apartment in Greenwich Village with a window box of basil instead of this teeming acreage, and never have to drive these hundreds of miles. As dawn moves into morning, I wonder if this might be the day she does not come down for breakfast. It is a game I play with myself, but soon I hear faucets running and bureau drawers opening.

AMERICAN SINGER

I uncover the cage where Godzilla, the yellow American Singer canary, sits on his swing, and carry it from the living room to the kitchen. He trills beautifully for minutes at a time, singing for a mate, a mate that will never arrive, just as poets and writers sit at their desks, hoping for an audience....

THAT'S CLASS

Richard Baker paints exact replicas of old paperbacks that include creased covers and dog-eared pages. His gallery once sold these literary paintings at half-price. They were still expensive, but the bargain was too hard to resist. My wife said, "You can't have just *one!*" and so both *A Century of Humorous Verse* and Françoise Sagan's *Bonjour Tristesse* greet me this morning. I add, "You can't have just one" to the list of my wife's possible epitaphs.

I like Richard's humor. He told me that a collector who treated him like a king put him up in a fancy hotel in Venice.

"In the bathroom, on each side of the toilet," he said, "was a dispenser holding rolls of paper. One on the left and one on the right. *That's class!*"

It's hard to leave Richard and his wit, but I must go, past my grandfather's oil painting, a copy of a Winslow Homer. My grandfather, a framer who owned the Museum Art Shop on Madison Avenue, was also a first-rate forger. If I had his gift, and larceny in my veins, I wouldn't be heading out the door to Boston. I'd be behind an easel adding to my bank account. If could draw the cover of a book instead of writing one, I'd be on a throne in Venice.

Life is but a dream!

Good-bye, grandfather! Farewell, Richard! *Bonjour, Tristesse!*

Tea For Two

A guest bathroom off the long hallway to the front door contains a tub, three feet deep, surrounded by sea-green tile. It's the Kohler model, "Tea for Two," and I have never stepped into it.

Yes, one can dream, but one dreams alone.

STEPS

Thoreau wrote, "Instead of having a dog to growl before your door, the Atlantic Ocean growls for a whole Cape!" But there is also a miniature Doberman, Gracie, in the next yard, tied to a tree, barking all day as she wraps and unwraps herself around its trunk, a commute similar to mine.

Kenny, a master carpenter, built these perfect porch steps, with low risers and wide treads. He rectified the original contractor's mistake: off-kilter, narrow and steep, by smashing them into shards with a maul, a tough task even for a muscular man accustomed to such work. On that day, Kenny brought along his sixteen-year-old son, Curtis, of whom he was very proud. The editor of his high-school literary magazine, *Hyacinths and Biscuits,* Curtis wanted to be a writer. My wife and I gave him copies of our books. As Kenny heaved that chunk of steel onto the wooden planks, I saw the boy on tiptoes, stretching his slender body over a rose bush so as not to disturb any branches, his spine forming a kind of balletic arc, almost a question mark, in order to smell a yellow blossom. The next day, Kenny told us that Curtis had fashioned a showcase from an old aquarium to display the books. Then he asked if we thought anything was wrong with his son. We said not at all, but Kenny said he was unsure. I could tell he wanted advice, but then he withdrew and said that although Curtis loved books as much as we did, he, himself, was not a reader, and Kenny went back to his work, raising the maul and yelling over his shoulder, "I'm a doer!"

ALLOW ME TO INTRODUCE HIMSELF

I needed a vehicle with all-wheel drive for the New England winter, and this Venza was the last one on the lot at Orleans Toyota. Before buying this car, I had just one citation: for going thirty mph in a twenty-five zone in Texas with New York plates, so the plates were to blame. And when I get a ticket, I am also not myself. The tickets go to a man who thinks of himself in the third person when he gets in trouble, or even dares trouble. You'll see more of him soon. He was an overachieving only child raised by overbearing parents. To go against their wishes, I used to say to myself, *And then he bought a gram of hash and hid it in the back of the sock drawer.* And later, I used it to avoid myself. I watched myself, as on a movie screen, and said the voice-over in my head: *And then he left The Sand Bar with Katie Pio, the tax assessor who slept with every civic employee and, when she finished with them, went through the volunteer fire department, with a special affection for the rescue squad.* Rather than be with Katie, I watched myself with her. I was the bearer of light and he followed me like a shadow. In fact, he was my shadow, and yet sometimes I followed him. I was a self-voyeur, a *voyeur moi-même.* The French do not call it that. I call it that, but he made it up.

I Thought I Heard a Young Man Crying

After wiping condensation from the windshield, I start the engine, and the radio coincidentally plays "Morning Dew." I once planned to use the lyrics from that song, "Thought I heard a young man crying / You didn't hear no young man crying," as an epigraph to my first book of poems, which I felt would diminish criticism of the collection as lovelorn self-pity, which it was.

Now I decide to use it in my next book.

Then I realize decades have passed.

It's too late—it's a young man's epigraph and that man is gone. Now it will be other men, young men, to deny they are crying. Older men in beach chairs in the shade have learned to keep their tears to themselves, or cry on the inside, as spiders are said to do.

INVISIBLE

Like an old whore—that's how my wife describes her acre of gardens in this early spring. Hydrangea stalks brown and spiky. The heads of sunflowers listing to the soil. All summer, company will arrive, and numerous, voluminous drinks will be served on the patio among phlox, loosestrife, and lilies with the names Scatterbrain and Miss Lucy. I have come to understand something about my wife and her garden. She spends all fall, part of the winter, and the entire spring on these beds. When they bloom, the fruit of her labor does not exist for her until friends and visitors see it.

Today, I won't exist for her either, or she for me, like paintings hung so long on a wall you don't see them anymore. I will disappear before her eyes and leave her here to the enchantment of yard work, work which conjures terraces of bulbs into blossom, bringing herself to life through the eyes of others.

In this way we are entirely different. I spend months writing, but as soon as it appears in a journal or a book—for me, it doesn't exist anymore. I know; it should be otherwise. Maybe I got this from Barthes, who said writing is that neuter, that composite where all identity is lost. More likely, I got it from my father. When I asked him what he would have been if he hadn't been an envelope salesman, he said he would have liked to have been invisible.

THE HOTTEST AND MOST INTELLIGENT

At the stop sign where my street, Overlook Drive, joins Sandy Lane, I see Cape Cod Bay in the distance, beyond the houses of the very rich on the promontory called Corn Hill. Mansions with multiple chimneys form a stark silhouette, and the blue water behind them flashes. Alan Dugan, Pulitzer Prize-winning poet, lived here in Truro and explained how Corn Hill got its name:

> After the Puritans landed at Provincetown
> and the women washed their dirty clothes,
> their men marched to Truro to perform
> their first political act: theft.
> They stole the Indians' corn
> buried on Corn Hill ...
> this country was made
> by a bunch of dirty crooks.

A neighbor jumps out of her house waving a book of mine, comes up to the car, and asks me to sign it. I don't really know her. I can't recall her name. I don't want to hurt her feelings. I have a solution. I say, "I forgot how to spell your name."

She says, "With an *e.*"

I stare ahead at the twinkling blue. Her husband, who had been working in the garden, joins us.

Finally, she says, "Carole."

I sign, "To Carole, a good friend and neighbor."

They read the inscription and her husband says, "How about adding, 'To the hottest woman on Overlook Drive?'" Carole looks annoyed and says, "I prefer 'the most intelligent woman on Overlook Drive.'"

I take the book, add *hottest* and *most intelligent* and drive off, trying to remember that this day is different, that everything that comes along is the best thing that could happen.

WHAT ARE DAYS FOR?

Carpenters putting a new roof on a house are singing because it's Friday. The radio is tuned to a hard rock station and every so often someone echoes a refrain. On Monday, only the sound of saws and hammering. Tuesday, low talk, sports scores. A little lifting of the heart on Wednesday, some laughter. Thursday brings a cacophony of joking, commands, and suggestions intoned with irony. Today, harmonizing, shouts of plans for the weekend and leaving the site a few minutes early. What are days for?

> Ah, solving that question
> Brings the priest and the doctor
> In their long coats
> Running over the fields.

Now

I know too well what this day is for—the English Department retreat. Classes have ended but last week, at the final department meeting, the chairman announced this eight-hour event and called on me to describe it to my colleagues. The grueling length doesn't matter. The promise of summer allows those who attend to endure anything, but the chair still likes to orchestrate an upbeat feeling. He chose me because in my twenty years at the college I have become known for my skill at comforting others in the face of empty exercises. I explained that the agenda would consist of committees reporting on the strengths and failures in the areas under their purview and I compared it to the Last Judgment, where some receive wings for angelic self-sacrifice, and others horns for putting their own work first.

The chairman asked if I could be more specific, so I recalled stopping by Jonathan Aaron's office before the session, so we could walk together to the conference room across campus. Jonathan had a bad cold. He told me it was from stress. Not stress from grading final exams and research papers, but stress from having published a new book of poems. The publisher had mangled his biographical note on the cover, omitting his college affiliation. Jonathan had sent a copy to the president, who replied with a scolding e-mail, saying that if he had touted his Emerson connection, she would have done for his book what she does for all faculty authors: purchase one hundred copies. Jonathan lost sleep over her response and, in the middle of the night, wrote her an e-mail saying he was sorry that the president of an institution of higher learning paid more attention to the outside of a book than to its contents. The next day, the morning of last year's retreat, he woke with a cold.

The college's new austerity plan had eliminated food and drink from the budget, so Jonathan and I stopped at George's Keystone Market to buy lunch. I ordered an Italian sub and Jonathan a pint of chicken soup. At our noon break, Jonathan was distressed to find that George had given him a fork instead of a spoon.

I told my colleagues that what I remember most about the retreat was watching Jonathan Aaron, hour upon hour, for the rest of that day, struggling to eat soup with a fork.

COYDOGS AND CHIGROES

I'm already behind schedule, but I pause for a second and think about turning right, toward Provincetown, land's end, where there is no time at all, where even a broken clock is wrong twice a day.

Over the winter, I took a drawing class there. At the first session, the teacher arrived late, entered the studio, and apologized.

"I'm sorry," she said. "The clock in my car is broken. And I don't have a clock in my house."

Maybe she was exaggerating. Everything gets exaggerated in Provincetown. Its citizen-inmates love to hear and invent fables. The Portuguese fishermen were great storytellers and mingled in bars and restaurants with artists and writers, matching them tale for tall tale. A few years ago, when coyotes started roaming the town, this peace-loving population said it was a natural phenomenon, live and let live. Then cats and small dogs started disappearing and rumors flew: a coyote den was discovered under town hall and, in it, a pile of bloody cat collars. Dog trainer and writer Debbie Doobie measured coyote carcasses and said they were oversized, concluding that the coyotes had been mating with German shepherds—we were dealing not with coyotes but *coydogs*. She said they had the strength of a dog and the wiles of a coyote. To prove her point, she cited the Chigroes in Ian Fleming's *Doctor No,* a race bred to have Chinese savvy and Negro brawn. She smoked a lot of grass, which is how she got her name.

Living in Provincetown leaves you unfit for living anywhere else in the world, including Provincetown.

ONLY ONE

There is only one city for everyone, just as there is only one major love.

GRAVES

A beckoning neon sign on the roof of a small shack simply says PACKAGE STORE. The road dips deeply here, and cell phones lose connections as if the slumping highway is telling drivers to end all communication and just swirl in, circle the drain so to speak, and stop for a snort. I used to call my father every Saturday at noon as I climbed out of this valley, loaded with gin for the weekend. After he died, I repeated my opening words as well as his on this weekend errand, a kind of reminiscence, a sort of remembrance, a certain relief.

"Hi, Dad."

"Hello, John. How are you?"

Then he'd recite his grocery list and sometimes tell me in his thin voice to buy for him twenty shares of stock in a company on a losing streak. A former airplane mechanic and envelope salesman with an eighth-grade education, he dabbled in the market with his minimal funds. "Buy on bad news, sell on good," was his guideline.

I say it now, "Hi, Dad."

I don't answer for him today because today he answers. He is warning me about the package store, to pass it by and not drink too much, saying that God provides just one liver per customer. He says he knows I've recently learned why he lost the house in Connecticut when I was in kindergarten—he was fired from several jobs due to repeated drunken-driving arrests. We had never discussed why our family of three returned to the railroad flat where I was born, above my grandmother's apartment in Queens, where she owned the building. It must have been a woeful reversion, this accepting of charity from his mother-in-law. My mother was crushed. She grew up in that Judge Street apartment, Olga Bertolotti, and became Olga Skoyles when she married my father. She felt like a different person entirely when she left, and she had to return, a new wife with a young child and a failed husband. She often spoke of the lost Connecticut house, the gravel driveway and her rock garden as if it were a dream, and it had turned out to be just that.

I became aware of my father's alcohol problem only after he died.

20

A friend who worked as a detective searched family records for his amusement and filled me in. I then realized my father must have been drunk those Sunday afternoons back in Queens when he fought with my mother after our midday dinner and suggested he and I go for a drive out to Long Island, to the home of Theodore Roosevelt. We took the Long Island Expressway and arrived in Oyster Bay where we followed signs I still remember, "To the Home of Theodore Roosevelt," signs we passed again and again. Why do I recall such a mundane and banal direction? Because it never led to our destination. We drove around the town, up and down hills, reading those signs but eventually returning to our own home where he immediately went to bed. His language on those trips was colorful, original, manic, saying, *N. O., Baby,* when I asked him to slow down, and warning me playfully that he'd give me a *Smash in the crash.* He was sipping something along the way from a soda bottle, but I never connected it to alcohol.

He comes along for the ride today because the dead don't stay where they're buried, they don't know what graves are for. I tell him he can join me on one condition, that he remain the late Gerard Skoyles, that disembodied voice on the phone, a voice only I can hear, a voice from the grave, and he's fine with that because it means today he gets his wish—he's invisible.

THE CASE

"What have you been doing since you died?"

"I thought I'd be lonely, but that isn't the case."

"I always liked it when you said, 'the case.'"

"Being dead is very much like being alive, really. And in some ways it's better because you're free of the fear of death. When life ends, death also ends."

"I'm not sure I get that," I say.

"It's like being a spectator at a game where you don't care who wins or loses."

"Can you be happy or sad?"

"There's a certain disappointment. At the moment I closed my eyes and knew I would never open them again, I felt some of my life was a missed opportunity."

"What would you have done differently?"

"I'd have done what I wanted. Take risks like the self-help books say. I might have made a living as a cartoonist, I had some talent. I also could have been a very good truck driver. I loved driving."

"It could be, Dad, that maybe you just liked getting away."

"I think you're right! Maybe it wasn't driving, maybe it was leaving."

"You were a good father, except when it came to my girlfriends."

"I wish I could make up for it."

"You taught me a lot. I have your book of quotations, which I love."

"I kept it for years."

"The cover is funny, remember? It says *Be a Fine and Dandy Fellow, Follow Through!*"

"I should have written down the authors of those quotes. I wish I'd done that."

"I liked *Only by avoiding the beginning of things, can we escape their ending.*"

"My favorite was *Today is the tomorrow I worried about yesterday.*

Don't worry too much, John. Soon your life will be yesterday."

"That could be true."

"Hey, keep your eyes on the road!"

My Wedding

Alan Dugan and Judy Shahn, a printmaker, were married for fifty years, living on Old County Road. Dugan dedicated each of his seven books to his wife and Judy designed every cover. My wife and I, inspired by the longevity of their romance and their union in the arts, married on their porch, but when we arrived for our wedding, Judy had just finished scrubbing black paint from the large screen slider of her studio where Dugan had written, "I hate you, you fucking cunt."

As a gift for hosting the affair and, since Judy was a serious cook, my wife brought her a shopping bag of exotic condiments from Bloomingdale's, among them an expensive bottle of vinegar, its cork a bundle of foil; salty caramels; French mustard, and a jar of balsamic jam. I gave Dugan a case of his favorite beer, Budweiser.

My best man did not show up. We had shared an apartment in P'town years earlier, and he called at the last minute to say there were too many ghosts around for him to handle. The justice of the peace pulled me aside and reminded me that she also served the town as parking clerk and I had several unpaid tickets.

After the JP pronounced us man and wife, Judy filled the champagne flutes, Dugan gave the toast, and the wedding party raised their glasses, drank, and went into fits of choking, coughing, and spitting, as Judy had served the vinegar by mistake.

U-Turn

"What are you doing?" my father asks when I make a quick U-turn at Long Nook Road, and swerve back toward Provincetown. My father has a great sense of direction when he's sober, and he's sober now.

"You'll see," I say.

He was also a great driving teacher, and taught me to drive in high school, choosing the perfect spot: the parking lot of the Steinway & Sons Piano Factory in Astoria. The vast asphalt expanse on Saturday mornings forgave awkward left turns and fishtailing in reverse. It is only now, as I write this, that I realize we used to stop at Tito's Liquor Emporium afterward where he'd spend a fortune and, at the checkout, buy me a Milky Way and a Chuckles.

"Remember when you taught me to drive, and Tito's?"

"Tito's had good value."

"The only place I saw you push a shopping cart."

As if an occult hand has control of my grasp on the wheel, I am heading for the town of no time and begin to daydream. I wish I had brought my Moby Grape CD, *Wow,* which propels my brain forward in a psychedelic roar still echoing from my hippie mescaline-and-methedrine-fueled days, and I would have forged ahead to Boston. Instead, Noel Coward croons from Pandora's shuffle station and sends me into a nostalgic mist:

> I'll see you again
> Whenever spring breaks through again.
> Time may lie heavy between,
> But what has been
> Can leave me never.

A GIRL FROM THE PAST

In Provincetown, I turn left off Bradford, go down Pearl, and park at the motel on the bay, the Bull Ring Wharf, where I used to live in the seventies. I scan the area for some sign of eternity and find it in the faces of two people for whom I have great affection: the managers, Jean and Bob Post. They ran the place for the two winters I stayed here. Their surname suggests stability as well as motion. They are both sixty years old, childhood sweethearts who moved from Maine and have come to resemble each other over the years: stocky builds, short gray hair, wearing T-shirts and shorts. Jean is fastidious with the reservation book and Bob can fix anything. Even in front of the television, he's twirling a screwdriver as if daring some mechanism to break.

Every Sunday in warm weather they invited me for French toast, which Mrs. Post served on the deck facing the bay. While we ate, she distributed sections of the *Cape Cod Times,* always asking Mr. Post for his preference. He replied, "Just the funnies. That's as intellectual as I want to get." Same answer, every week. And he did read them, and then worked the Jumble with a flat carpenter's pencil.

Mr. and Mrs. Post died a decade ago, but I am here with them today.

Mrs. Post is disappointed in me. Mr. Post never said much, but I can tell he agrees with his wife by the way he stares across the water to the lighthouse on Long Point. And after all these years, I have come to believe she was right, I made a mistake.

In the spring of 1979, when I was teaching at Southern Methodist University in Dallas, I flew to Provincetown for a meeting to judge the manuscripts for writing fellowships at the Fine Arts Work Center, where I had been a fellow myself. I brought a girlfriend, Anne. She was my student and twenty years old. I was her teacher and twenty-five. Anne was energetic, lively, and bookish. Although I was five years her senior, she seemed older, as if she had broken through the eggshell a few days before me and was up and around. By using that metaphor,

I know I'm expressing a kinship that means a kind of sister, or even brother because there was also a boyishness about her, as forceful as any man when she joked at a bar, yet her overall presence was a robust and beckoning femininity. Her mother's love had infused her with the gift of self-confidence, the feeling of a conqueror which Freud believed a favorite child retains for life. As for me, my parents loved me just as much but, an only child, I had no rivals, so I created out of my imagination weak siblings, paper dolls made of words.

While I attended the manuscript meetings, Anne helped Mrs. Post fold towels, sweep sand from the guest rooms, and mix exotic drinks in her new blender. At the end of our stay, Mrs. Post took me aside and said, "Don't let her get away, John."

I was raised by my parents to do what I'm told, a command reinforced by Dominican nuns, Christian brothers, and, in college, the Jesuits. And I have always obeyed. But a year later, I left Dallas, and Anne and I parted ways.

She was twenty and I was twenty-five. Student and teacher. I'm ashamed of myself, but he's not. I was her teacher and he was her lover, and now I return to the motel, the stage on which Mrs. Post told me what to do, ordered me, in fact, with the best and most heartfelt of intentions. Her words haunt me, but haunt is too blithe a word for this landlord's charge which I would have forgotten if not that a few months ago I heard from Anne, now fifty-seven to my sixty-two. A message in my e-mail inbox intrigued me with its subject line: *A Girl from your Past*. She had discovered a poem of mine in the *New Yorker* while helping her teenage daughter with a literature project. Still living in Dallas, Anne had become a lawyer and an accomplished painter of watercolors.

Now she is standing at the office door, an overnight bag at her feet, Mr. and Mrs. Post smiling behind her, waiting for me to pick her up for the ride to Boston. Not that she doesn't have a car; she does, she has a Mercedes SUV like the wealthy soccer mom she is, but she needs a lift from the past to the present, and I am happy to accommodate this ghost no one will see but me. At last, she's completely mine. I should be ashamed of myself, but he's not. I'm the married man, but he's single and now I open the passenger door and she enters, filling the car with a familiar fragrance: *I Dreamt the Past Was Never Past Redeeming.*

THE ACTUAL AND THE IMAGINARY

If you were to see us driving along in my Venza, you wouldn't see her at all unless you painted her with a bucket of that stuff they sell at the Juju shops in New Orleans that makes the invisible apparent. Then you'd see her—pressing the AC buttons on the dashboard, searching for an all-news station to get the forecast, rummaging through a knapsack of books—but you wouldn't see her as she was then. Only I can see her that way. You'd see a worn blonde with a crooked mouth and deep brown eyes, weighing one hundred and ten pounds, for whom I've turned around to take on this trip where the actual and the imaginary meet and each imbues the other with its opposite characteristic.

EVERYWHERE PRESENT AND NOWHERE VISIBLE

Every so often I'd come across photographs I took of Anne: opening a bottle of Heineken against her hip; reading by a waterfall in western Massachusetts; in front of my parents' New York apartment wearing a tailored blue dress, my arm around her, my hairline receding, and my forehead sweating.

My mother used to say, "Opposites attract," and although we were alike when it came to our interior lives, we were opposites in many ways. She hiked, rode a bike long-distance, jogged. I had played only one outdoor sport: dominoes in a café in the west village. My mother judged the girlfriends I brought home: "So-and-so is not my type," and "So-and-so is more my type." *My type.* The words conjured up the image of that captive gorilla who loved cats. When presented with a book of photographs, he pointed seriously to his choice: a Manx. *His type.* That's what I think of now when I hear *my type:* an ape cuddling a kitten.

Our recent e-mail exchange focused on what we were reading as well as Anne's work in watercolor. She mentioned that the *New Yorker* made her think of John Cheever, and she had just read *A Trip to Echo Spring,* about alcoholic writers, which included him and Raymond Carver. I told her I had known both of them in graduate school at the Iowa Writers' Workshop, but that I wasn't much interested in the topic of that book. "It's a little too close to home for me," I wrote. "I'm always trying to cut down on the Martinis, but they only get bigger and stronger."

She replied that she, too, could not have read that book a few years ago, that she had had some issues with alcohol, was genetically hard-wired for it, but hadn't taken a drink in over ten years. She apologized for taking the fun out of the exchange and hoped she hadn't been too serious.

I thought back to our time together in Dallas: we drank pitchers of margaritas and frequented liquor stores that in those days had drive-through windows. When the clerk handed over the bottle, he included "go cups"—plastic tumblers of ice. We didn't actually eat much on our dates, just drank. When I'd offer to order dinner, she'd say, "No, I'll just be a fish," and so would I.

I told her about the memoir I'd recently published, *A Moveable Famine,* which covered, among other things, my days as a student in Iowa. She said the book sounded as if it was mostly about drinking. I said no, not really, but then I paged through it with her words in mind.

I was shocked. It *was* all about drinking.

I asked if we could talk. Our conversation showed me how alcohol had dictated my daily life. The next week, I stopped drinking, cold turkey, free from deciding each day what I was going to eat that would provide a serious foundation for my three hours of dry Martinis in the evening and into the night. I was relieved from the burden of gauging the minutes so I would be at my liquor cabinet at exactly six p.m. and furious if something intervened.

To clarify this for myself, I wrote an essay about Anne getting in touch, realizing my book's subject, and being in the dark about it for decades. I described driving with Ray Carver in his old Ford Falcon and, one morning, after a long stretch of barhopping into the early hours, Ray phoned and asked if we had had an accident the night before. The most I could say was that I didn't think so. He said he couldn't understand it, that when he woke up, he found one side of his car caved in. "Cheever and I could hardly get it together today to call a cab to take us to the liquor store," he said. Cheever, too, drank heavily then, and at a party one night we all stared with concern as he danced alone in the living room, after numerous Martinis and as many glasses of wine, his hand over his heart.

My stories were mainly about the follies and tragedies of getting smashed: like cruising around Malibu, thinking I had two flat tires on the same side of my car, stopping, getting out, and realizing I'd been driving with two wheels on the curb. Or my friend who kept a chart of every two-for-one drink night in his city; the one who gashed his forehead walking into a stop sign; another maimed by a train as he drank on the rails.

Though my memoir recorded a famine of nutrition, funds, and fame, it documented how thirst always found a way to be quenched. Sometimes, at cocktail hour at my house, my friends would take an eight-ounce measuring cup, fill it with water, and pour it into my empty oversize Martini glass, which held it all, no lip room, just to show the staggering amount of alcohol that went into my drinks. It always got a big laugh. Two of those enormous Martinis would start the evening.

I discovered the same subject at the heart of my books of poems. One piece, "Saturday Night with my Dead Friends," has me pouring drinks for those now gone: Alan Dugan, Larry Levis, and Michael Sheridan. I even refer to myself as "their understudy" as I raise a toast to their ghosts.

I put Anne in this car because I don't hear from her often, although last week she sent a note telling me to read an article in the Sunday *Times* on the feel-good gene, which alcoholics lack and make up for through booze. I held the paper in front of me and I could see her hands holding the column, and imagined her eyes trained on the text, the text before me, the page she read two thousand miles away. An invisible bond that also would link me to more than a million others, but when I thought of her reading that same paper, the letters rose from the newsprint and floated like a veil, a veil I wanted to lift to see her face. I had no choice but to take her with me.

DOWNTOWN

At the sign for Downtown Truro, Anne asks me to stop. Downtown consists of the post office, Mac's fish store, and Jam's Gourmet, a specialty shop known for what the *Boston Globe* called, "eye-popping prices and employees who can't seem to smile." We must pick up our mail because the town is too small to warrant home delivery. Postal workers are driven mad in the summer when the population rises from 1,700 to 30,000. Last August, an overworked clerk quit, but not before flinging his ring of keys and hitting a customer in the throat. Letters are routinely placed in the wrong box, late fees accumulate on bills, insurance policies are canceled, and workers who don't throw keys look like the idea has crossed their minds.

"Remember those crazy envelopes?" I ask my father.

"They were a lot of fun," he says. "Except for the one I sent to the IRS."

My father worked most of his life at 125th and Amsterdam Avenue in Harlem for the Connecticut Valley Paper and Envelope Company. One day he was doodling during a meeting and his boss admired his silhouette of a large-breasted woman and had it printed on stationery. It sold well and my father drew others: a trapeze artist midair, about to grasp the outstretched hands of his partner; a crowd moving in one direction, and a forlorn, shadowy pedestrian going the other. And his biggest hit: an envelope featuring a pink tiger with black stripes, sitting on a barrel marked TNT. The tiger has a cigar in his mouth and is about to strike a match on the keg. My father blamed being audited on using this one to file his tax return.

Anne shows me the novelty postcards she's mailing: a clam tree with shellfish in its branches, a huge striped bass on a flatbed truck, a goosefish choked to death trying to swallow a large codfish. They are all addressed to her deceased mother. Anne says, "She's not dead on this trip," and gets out of the car.

I sit behind the wheel and say to myself, "No one's dead on this trip. On this trip, everyone's alive, especially the dead."

MAIL ART

Ray Johnson *is* dead. He killed himself in 1995.

The creator of the New York Correspondance School (sic), Ray Johnson sent what his estate calls, "chopped-up collages; drawings with instructions ('please add to and return ...'); found objects; snakeskins; plastic forks; and annotated newspaper clippings" through the post office to friends, fellow artists, and critics. A collector once offered to buy a piece of Johnson's for 75 percent of the asking price. Johnson agreed, and then chopped off a quarter of the canvas. He shunned the spotlight until he became "the most famous unknown artist in New York."

A friend of mine sent me an imitation of Johnson's trademark cartoon bunny in tribute to him. In return, I decided to address an envelope to Johnson's last residence near Sag Harbor where he committed suicide by drowning. Knowing the post office would return it as undeliverable, I planned to use the envelope to make a little collage for my friend. But it slipped my mind and I never sent the letter. Then one day, I was paying bills and remembered. I wrote Ray Johnson's address on an envelope and went to the post office. I dropped the letters into the box and opened the large drawer that holds my mail—to see Ray Johnson's face staring up at me. He was on the cover of *The Believer*, with the subtitle—"Return to Ray Johnson."

He's still making mail art, even from this distance, from his life that ended in 1995 to mine, in 2018.

Ray Johnson *is not* dead.

THE DUMP DANCE

I throw a bag of trash into the hopper at the transfer station. I don't have time to visit The Swap Shack, where citizens leave and take books, clothes, glassware, and utensils. A sign hangs on its door, painted by a dyslexic patriot after 9/11: *Untied We Stand.*

The Dump Dance used to be held here at the close of Truro Treasures weekend, a Sunday night in September. Each town on the Outer Cape has its own event: every autumn there is the Wellfleet Oyster Festival as well as Orleans's "Fall for Orleans." And each spring, Brewster celebrates itself with a floral "Brewster in Bloom" gala. This year's theme is "Clamoring for Clams." Eastham's Chamber of Commerce touts its Turnip Festival, noting: *Turnip madness and mayhem returns!* Provincetown has no need for a singular event because it is one continuous carnival where madness and mayhem don't return because they never leave.

The dance at the dump was the climax of two days of bicycle and tricycle races, face painting, flea markets, arts and crafts fairs, and best-pet contests. Everyone brought bottles of liquor and coolers of beer and set up folding chairs, getting drunk while listening to a female folk singer who, in an effort to rouse the crowd, often twisted her guitar behind her back so she could clap her hands over her head. Although the hopper was empty, the scent of rotten vegetables and sour milk drifted over the gathering. In a way, the 9/11 sign was prescient: everyone was untied and they stood, but not for long. Most nodded off in their lawn chairs.

When my son was ten, he wanted to join the party at the dump, so we went, first stopping for dinner at Guido Bandito, a new Mexican restaurant in downtown Truro, where we sat at a table by the window. A huge Harley on the bar left only two stools, which were occupied by an arguing couple. The horrible enchiladas either perfectly imitated a frozen TV dinner or were the thing itself. Horrible, too, were the couple's angry words, which ended in the woman's final crescendo delivered as she slid off the barstool, pointed her finger at her partner and, before walking out, said, "Fuck you. Fuck you. Fuck you. Fuck you. Fuck you." My son looked at me, and I said what any academic father would say: "Ten-syllable line." After dinner, we were turned away from the dump because a drunk had run over the toe of the policeman directing traffic. The injured cop was rushed to Cape Cod Hospital by the Rescue Squad and police shut down the dance, sending all the tipsy drivers home at once, which resulted in a dozen fender-benders.

MERCY, MERCY, MERCY

A bright black BMW with the vanity plate LVING LIFE pulls up to the Swap Shack as I'm leaving, and a gray-haired man gets out of the passenger side carrying a toaster he's going to donate. Suddenly, his car's headlights and interior lights flash madly and a siren sounds. The man spins around and screams at the woman behind the wheel. He makes wild instructive motions at the windshield, gestures meaning "turn the key" and "press buttons." With a confounded look, the woman rolls down the window of this obviously new car in order to hear him. As I drive past, I see he is furious, tossing the toaster to the ground and pulling her out of her seat by the arm. Does the plate mean *Living* or *Loving?* Probably not loving. In my rearview mirror, I see him continuing to rage, accompanied by his car's rage.

I wait to turn onto Route 6 behind another new car, a white Mustang convertible, this one driven by someone with his arm out the window, fingers tapping the roof to a beat. These plates read *RAY C*—a man both living and loving life—my friend Ray Calano, a fishmonger until he hit the lottery for ten million. Over dinner years ago he told me he will never eat fish, the result of having worked in the industry for so long. When I asked why, he said that when the shop bought one hundred pounds of scallops from a boat on a Monday, they'd throw them into a tub of water laced with a chemical called STP, and on Tuesday—boom!—one hundred fifty pounds of scallops! Ray zips away, living and loving life. He attributes his windfall to the grace bestowed on him by Saint Pantaleon, whose image hangs from the Mustang's mirror by a silver chain.

Pantaleon, patron saint of raffles and whose name means *Mercy for Everyone,* be with me today!

John Skoyles

GENERATIONS

It is said there are three sexes: male, female, and Ray Calano's daughters, Shaylin and Nicole, who pull alongside me at the stoplight at Marconi Station. I would wave, but you don't look at Ray's daughters; in fact, you try not to look at them. Or you figure out a way to do so without burning your eyes, the way one views an eclipse. They are impossible to see without desire. A wave of heat creeps over the face of the most reserved man. I don't have to worry today as Shaylin has slammed her foot to the gas and zoomed ahead.

"Those are the most beautiful girls around," I tell my father.

"Nothing compared to the Burke twins," he says. "They danced at the Latin Quarter. Jackie Burke could rotate one breast in one direction and the other in the opposite direction."

"Didn't her daughter go to Saint Barth's, a few years ahead of me? Mindy Burke?"

"Yes, she did, but I never heard of her doing anything like that. It must skip a generation."

38

IRON MAN

According to his obituary in the *Provincetown Advocate,* Joseph "Iron Man" Francis, Provincetown's most renowned drunk, got his name from bending the inch-thick bars on a jail cell door. John F. Noons hired him as the watchman at his excavation-and-junked-cars site in Truro. At one time Iron Man left town to join the circus, where his job was to walk on glass, but he was fired for getting drunk with the dancing bear and the bear's trainer. For years, he guarded tons of gravel, blue stone, and mulch, and slept among them in a Mustang without wheels.

I spent an hour with Iron Man while having my oil changed at Duarte's Motors. He told me that his parents came from such a poor and barren part of Portugal that on Christmas the children received an ice cream bar, a kind of Eskimo Pie, which they divided three ways, but they had no knife and cut it with a piece of wire kept on a nail on the wall. And that when they hanged criminals in that town, they had to take the bodies down quickly to hang the next because there was only one tree.

My son and his friends from grammar school often explored that junkyard, playing among the mulch piles, rusty springs, and shards of mirrors. They soon discovered that Iron Man's immobile car overflowed with pornographic magazines. When he was off at another part of the pit, they climbed into the Mustang and sat there propelled by fantasy, going nowhere and everywhere.

NORMAL

Anne sorts through the mail we picked up in Truro. Among various bills are two local papers, the *Cape Codder* and the *Advocate*. She opens the latter to the obituaries and reads aloud: Clifford Osgood, seventy-eight, owner of Small Treasures, an estate jewelry store, kept three Shih Tzus and, when he walked them from bar to bar, he was greeted by friends with, "Here he comes, three Shih Tzus to the wind." The obit ends, "No one knew if he was gay although he acted rather queenie."

My father says, "If you want to live in a normal town with a decent paper, there are thousands to choose from."

There is construction on Route 6, and I awkwardly navigate among Jersey barriers, parked trucks, police cars and flag men, and I tell Anne I might need a cataract operation.

My father yells, "Take your distance on the left!" which brings me back to the Steinway piano company lot, hearing that command which I never did understand.

I enjoy the cozy journalism of the P'town paper which suits the town's fantastic storytelling. A few days ago, a horse threw its rider as they rode down the beach, the horse continuing into town where it collided with a vehicle. The police report described the cause of the accident as "galloping the wrong way on Commercial Street."

Last week, when a bicyclist lay unconscious on the trail in the Beech Forest, his bright orange Baltimore Orioles baseball cap at his side, every person in the crowd had a theory.

"He got hit by those fat guys going really fast. I bet they did it."

"I got tripped up here last week. A wild turkey ran into my spokes."

"Maybe it was a fox. They're everywhere now."

"There's an albino fox in town. It's blind."

"And deaf!"

The police and an ambulance arrived. The crowd grew. A cop asked what happened. Someone said, "A Baltimore oriole landed on his cap and knocked him off his bike." The policeman, nodding thoughtfully, made a note which appeared in his report and was printed in the paper.

Today a bird mates with a hat.

Yesterday, a homeless man arrested for shoplifting will be rumored to be the descendant of the king who invented drawn butter.

Last week, a woman who tripped outside the Old Colony Tap at closing time and cut her forehead became two murdered actresses.

Tomorrow, a man who left the Cape in the morning for Boston will be cited for driving by himself in the High Occupancy Vehicle lane on Route 93 and will swear he is not alone.

NOT ALONE

I have a persistent image of her. She's in the shower, having just rinsed her blonde hair which streams back, fully exposing her face, her drenched hair now a little darker from the water. Her breasts rise as she smooths her scalp with her palms, over her head and down her neck. As she does, she knows I'm staring, and she smiles, pleased, almost happy, maybe proud of herself. Behind her, a soap dish set into the tile wall, and an orange cake of Dial that washed so long ago down the drain. This memory stands for a time I loved, because I loved her then. That smile worried me somewhat, because I thought it was for herself, a delight in her youth and beauty, not because of my presence. I could have been a mirror, a camera, or any man, or maybe not.... I can't understand that smile, which is what I recall most, that, and my staring at her, and never breaking away, even now.

FRIENDS IN HIGH PLACES

The Psychohistory Group's annual conference of world-famous political thinkers, writers, and psychiatrists meets at Robert Jay Lifton's Wellfleet house on Ocean View Drive. One afternoon is open to the community. The first time I attended, Lifton's wife, B. J., saw me enter, a bit lost, and she kindly beckoned me to a seat in the front row, directly before the two speakers, Daniel Ellsberg, the distributor of the Pentagon Papers, and Robert Kuttner, editor of the *American Prospect*. The men on each side of me introduced themselves: Jonathan Schell and Jeremy Rifkin, and we shook hands. I shook hands as well with someone else: Lady Jingly-Jones, the Liftons' white, coiffed standard poodle, who sat down directly in front of me, put out her paw, which I took and proceeded to hold for the next hour as I listened to the fate of the world.

A CHARMED LIFE

Edmund Wilson, the man of letters, lived on Money Hill Road in Wellfleet. His second wife, Mary McCarthy, wrote a novel about the town, *A Charmed Life,* saying, "You could not take a drink without wondering whether you might become an alcoholic. There was something sinister in the fact that you could not get anything repaired. There was nobody to fix the clock; the man who sharpened lawn mowers had died during the summer and nobody had succeeded him; the local laundry service could not clean a suit without tearing and discoloring it; the garage-man's only accomplishment was the ability to scratch his head. Everything in the village was relentlessly running down, buckling, warping, mildewing—including the human beings ... the gay, smart wives, mottled and bedizened, fantastically got up with shawls and peasant bangles—when two of them got together they made the First National check-out look like a fortune-tellers' convention."

My father is right; there are thousands of other, normal towns.

A MANHATTAN IN QUEENS

"You taught me to make a Manhattan when I was twelve."

"I did not!" my father says.

"Yes, you did. It was after I won second place in the spelling bee and we came home from Brooklyn Prep and Mom was visiting Uncle Dominic."

"You have some imagination."

"I was mad at myself for missing the word *impetus*. I spelled it *impetous*. I have a good memory."

"You were too young for hard liquor."

"You gave me the shaker, and I filled it with ice. I knew where the jigger was, and you got the Four Roses from the closet and the vermouth from the refrigerator. You told me three-to-one."

"I remember teaching you the difference between a dry and a sweet Manhattan. I remember that."

"For you, I poured three shots of rye over the ice and added a jigger of vermouth. You said I should make mine weaker, so I poured two ounces of rye and one ounce of vermouth for myself and shook it up."

"You're crazy!"

"You were laughing because it was all coming out the same."

"Yes, it would all come out the same."

"I drank two of them."

"You're crazy!"

KEYS

She was in my class and caught my attention on the first day when the student next to her didn't have the anthology and Anne moved her book and offered to share, a small spontaneous gesture. And when she spoke, every feature on her face seemed involved. I found myself looking at her, her eyes wide, as if absorbing the room, making everyone disappear, including me.

I wanted to see her outside of class, but how? I hoped she might linger after the others filed out, but no, she was too efficient, too self-possessed to dawdle, and always gathered her papers and books and left quickly. One day as I was walking up the stairwell, she was coming down. We talked on the landing for a moment and then continued the conversation in my office. A week later, I returned from a committee meeting and found her sitting there in a jogging outfit. She told me she had been out for a run and said, "I thought I'd stick my head in," which I found charming. We made a date for drinks on the weekend.

We met at Chelsea Corners. At one point she asked me to take off my glasses. I wore glasses with huge dark frames, long out of fashion. I bought them at a discount optometrist on Fourteenth Street in New York where a drunken panhandler saw me and said, "Get a load of Harold Lloyd!" Now I felt like him when she asked me to remove them, and I looked at her looking at the glasses through which I had looked at her. We went to several bars and ended up at the Jersey Lily until closing, when I drove her back to her car outside the Chelsea. But when we got there, she couldn't find her keys. Through the bar's front window, we saw the stacked chairs and, on our table, her ring of keys. She said she could stay at my place. I didn't want to have sex with her because of this accidental circumstance. So we slept together, but apart. The next morning we picked up her keys and she got into her car, but today she's in this one, the one running on fumes.

FATHER AND SON

Businesses around this harbor include The Wellfleet Actors Theatre, Pearl Café, The Bookstore Restaurant, and a pier friendly to fishermen where I took Harry when he was ten and we got our first rods and tackle.

I asked an old man who was catching large blues if my lure with its tiny hook was too small to land a big fish.

"Does an elephant eat a peanut?" he said.

I thanked him and as we walked away, my son asked, "Was that rude, Dad? Was he being rude?" I told him it was fisherman humor.

I set Harry up with a lure and he flung his line in the water. I walked twenty feet across the pier and did the same. The incoming tide, the old man told me, was a good time to fish. And it immediately seemed so—Harry and I simultaneously felt a tug on our lines and simultaneously yelled, "I got one!" We reeled in, fighting the strong resistance, which grew stronger and stronger, until I realized the current had taken my line under the wharf where it hooked up to his and we had caught each other.

A PARTY BOAT

I ask my father, "Remember, Dad, when we fished on party boats out of Sheepshead Bay?"

"I remember."

"Remember when I won the pool?"

He just smiles. Everybody chipped in a few dollars. At the end of the day, the one with the largest fish, decided by weight, took home the money.

I had caught a big fluke and felt sure I would win. When we docked, my fish was up against a smaller but compact mackerel. The mate weighed each and the mackerel proved heavier. It was a thick fish, but it was hard to believe. It was so hard to believe that my father grabbed the mackerel, slit open its belly, and several sinkers dropped out. The guy who caught the mackerel insisted the fish must have swallowed them. The crew guffawed, and my father took the money, tipped the mate, and handed the rest of the cash to me.

"That was great," I say.

THE LAST RESORT

Riley Clark, master mechanic, runs Clark Auto and is also a master of novelty songs which he sings throughout the day.

> Down around the Port o' Spain
> Lives Senorita What's Her Name.
> Fellas come and fellas go
> They come real fast but they go real slow.

When the *Boston Globe* asked me to write a profile of a local Cape character, I chose Riley. The editor was enthused about my account of Riley's honesty, sense of humor, and iconoclasm. I went to work right away but, in researching Riley, I found that before moving here, he served time in New Hampshire for turning back the odometers of a thousand cars.

I switched to a safe subject, a charming old woman, a native, slightly dotty, who painted primitive scenes of sailboats on the bay. After the article appeared, friends told me this woman had been a significant cocaine dealer, a fact known to all the locals. I delivered copies to her and brought up the subject. She said yes, she had been busted, and the worst part was that the police confiscated the morphine she had hoped to use to kill herself in her later years. "Why do you think they call this place The Last Resort," she said.

DEAR

In the first week of my sobriety, Anne texted me her phone number and said to call if I felt in danger of drinking. I never did, I was doing fine on my own, without a sponsor or meetings, but one late afternoon before hosting a dinner party, I felt ready to crumble. It wasn't the Beefeater gin I moved from the cabinet to the counter. It wasn't the cool green bottle of Stock Vermouth. It was the jar of olives that got to me. I pictured the olive on a toothpick in a glass of frigid gin, the glass chilled, a scrim of ice floating on the surface....

I dialed her number and I was trembling as I did, and not just from the fear of taking a drink.

She answered on the first ring, "Hello, dear."

Was Anne trying to revive our romance, now decades old? Or was she addressing me the way a nurse addresses a pathetic patient, to calm his nerves? In that moment of trying to get my bearings, I realized I wanted her to call me *dear.* As I was being sucked back through decades, as through a vortex, she said, "Oh, I'm sorry. I thought you were my husband."

That night I had a dream:

I'm walking down a street in a strange neighborhood when I see a house on fire, flames coming out the windows. I pound on the door and yell to those inside. I scream to neighbors to call the police, to call the fire department. Cars stop and people are arriving. Then I realize I'm naked! And then I realize that no one is paying any attention to my nakedness due to the fire.

PJ'S, JP'S, PB, AND JB'S

Those are the names of restaurants on Route 6 in Wellfleet, all within two miles of each other. They cater mostly to the summer people, the owners of second homes. Compared to the chambermaids, waiters, plumbers, carpenters and electricians, they are magical people, wispy and ghost-like. They feed the economy but stir resentment as they fly down the road in BMWs, Jaguars, and Porsches. The resentment toward them is so great that Provincetown and Truro have installed a two-tier property tax system: one for year-rounders and a higher levy for the summer populace.

My friend, a landscaper for decades, said he splurged on tickets to the Payomet Performing Arts Center to hear Delbert McClinton and was surprised his expensive seats were way in the back. He and his wife were the only locals. That would have been okay, he said, but he claimed the ears of the wealthy vacationers in the front rows absorbed most of the music and by the time it reached him it was just a faint trace of sound.

VERY FRENCH

The class divide is best seen at two Wellfleet venues: the PB Boulangerie and Cumberland Farms. I often visit them in tandem to get French bread for dinner and ice cream for dessert. Gray-haired men with younger women in designer clothes and sunglasses make up the long line at the bakery for baguettes, brioche, and croque monsieurs. I overheard a couple telling a friend about the high-quality horsehair blankets they bought for their two labradoodles. The man said they also purchased beautiful necklaces for the dogs.

"Collars," the wife corrected him. "Collars."

Fragrant smoke from chunks of cherry wood burning on an outside brasero wafts over the customers. Cumberland Farms, just two miles away but a world apart, is surrounded by fumes from the gas pumps. Inside, men wearing baseball caps buy lottery tickets, cigarettes, and milk. One holds a handful of ice to his cheek. The trucks outside display bumper stickers that say *If It's Tourist Season Why Can't We Shoot Them* and *Fuck You, You Fucking Fuck.*

I once had dinner at the Boulangerie. A dozen oysters cost thirty dollars and the server confused the drink order, then the rest of the order. And that happened all at once and at every table. Many men appeared from the back, some in white, each saying in a French accent with certain authority that he would straighten it out. Different mistaken appetizers and entrees then replaced the original wrong ones, with renewed promises. Everything was wrong, but everything was delicious. Everyone was in charge, and no one was doing anything. Very French.

I'm listening to Pierre Boulez's *Notations* as I'm passing the Boulangerie. When Boulez was asked why the tempo of the piece on the score is slower than when he conducts it, Boulez said, "When I compose, I cook with water, when I conduct, I cook with fire." Also very French. And something like the Boulangerie: when they cook, they cook with fire, but when they serve, they cook with water.

I am between the two worlds, and in my own world, the one my mother used to condemn me for living in. I can still hear her today, saying, "You're in your own world!" She wanted me, and my father, and everyone else, to be in hers. Maybe that's why I have chosen to drive the theoretical highway with a fantasy beside me more real than those who are alive.

"Right, Dad?"

"Whatever you say, John."

That's what he said when he didn't understand me, and he doesn't understand me now, which is why he mostly listens. If he could put into words what he is thinking, he would confide that experience improves life because you learn from it, while it simultaneously makes life worse, because you had to go through it.

THE WANDERING JEW

My father read one book all his life, and he never finished it: Eugène Sue's *The Wandering Jew,* whose fifteen hundred pages he kept by an armchair. Walter Benjamin criticized it in the *Arcades Project,* saying, "A novel is not a place one passes through; it is a place one inhabits." He was referring to the abundance of characters who appear and disappear. My father inhabited that book for decades, and now he is passing through this one.

Thomas Disch said of *The Wandering Jew,* "It has everything: an heiress falsely accused of madness and incarcerated in a lunatic asylum; a destitute hunchbacked seamstress of the highest moral character hopelessly in love with a blacksmith (who is a patriotic poet on the side); bloodthirsty panthers, telepathic twins, debauchery, murder, suicide, duels, supernatural manifestations, blazing passions, wild mobs, a plague of cholera, scenes in Java and the Arctic, the two best Reading of the Will scenes that ever were, and, towering over all these attractions, the nastiest crew of villains ever brought together in one book, presided over by the fiendish, the insidious, the wholly diabolic Jesuit priest and arch-hypocrite, Père Rodin, who is hell-bent on becoming the next pope."

How did my father acquire this volume? As a present from the sales manager at Connecticut Valley. The same boss insisted he read the *New York Times* and *New Ways to Greater Word Power.* My mother referred to Sue's novel as being very "deep" and when my father was reading, she would not disturb him and announced it the next day to everyone she met, saying, "Gerry's been reading. *The Wandering Jew.*" It meant nothing to me and less to our neighbors who were policemen, chauffeurs, steamfitters, longshoremen, and bartenders.

To supplement Disch's appraisal, I checked comments by readers on Amazon but found only one: "For the past twenty years I have tried to read a book a week so imagine my surprise when I received *The Wandering Jew.* I don't know what typeface is used but it is much too light. Coupled with the small type size, it makes it impossible for me to read the first page, much less the entire book. Even with my reading glasses, I cannot make out the words."

Even with my reading glasses, I cannot make out my father.

COFFEE, ETC.

On every trip I must drink coffee, but if I drink coffee, I will have to stop along the road in the men's rooms of Burger King, Dunkin' Donuts, and McDonald's. If I don't drink coffee, I will remain in a half-conscious state behind the wheel, and somewhere I will ask myself where I am going.

Every one of my friends my age has to pee a lot, not with the stream of youth, like a race horse, but in Morse code's elliptical dots and dashes.

Like those who take comfort when they share the fate of the great and famous in the most incidental way, I was reassured to read Norman Mailer's account of attending a memorial service at Saint John the Divine, getting there with difficulty, using two braces, and being seated in the front pew right before the altar. And then realizing he had to take a piss. He noted that with age there is a short distance between having to pee and peeing. He had no choice but to rise in full view of the congregation and sneak into an empty side chapel. When he entered, he saw Philip Roth and asked what he was doing.

Roth said, "I had to take a piss."

LIVING

At a rest stop, I ask Anne to show me her paintings. She opens her iPad to watercolors of bright red and yellow foliage surrounding rooftops in a village, and portraits of young girls, none smiling. She scrolls through these to her new work—shockingly different—crabs dancing around a frowning brain; a distraught pebble trapped in a teardrop.

I ask about this dramatic shift. She says that one morning, cleaning up the breakfast dishes, she walked onto her deck and flung the remains of her daughter's cereal bowl to the compost heap below, as she always did. But on this day, the milk splashed against a tree, and two cheerios stuck to the bark, giving the trunk eyes, so the oak seemed to be looking back at her, which she took as a sign to bring the inanimate to life.

"The way I've done with you," I say.

"If you call this living," she says.

ABOVE GROUND AND UNDERGROUND

One Sunday afternoon in Wellfleet, a woman yells out her window to kids playing Johnny-Ride-the-Pony, "Would you boys please keep it down! Justin's father is working on a book review, and I'm sure many of your fathers are also writing book reviews." The sons of carpenters and handymen understand nothing and continue their jostling.

Later that week, Justin's father meets the man from E-Z Doze It in front of his house.

Justin's father: I'm not sure where the septic tank is located, we've never had it pumped.

E-Z Doze It: I can find the lid with this probe.

He holds up a metal pole in the shape of a T.

Justin's father: Be careful. There's an expensive irrigation system here. Try not to puncture the hose.

He shows the man approximately where the line runs.

E-Z Doze It: No problem.

The tank is found, the lid removed, and waste sucked into the truck. Three hundred dollars.

That evening, Justin's father's irrigation system's warning bell sounds at the time the sprinklers come on, meaning a zone is broken. He calls E-Z Doze It and complains. The septic man says it's not his fault, Justin's father says it is, and they go back and forth before Justin's father loses his temper.

Justin's father: What kind of moron are you? I showed you the line, you seemed to understand, but obviously it was over your head. How you stay in business is beyond me.

E-Z Doze It: Sir, I have a question for you.

Justin's father: Yes?

E-Z Doze It: Can you see underground?"

Justin's father: What?

E-Z Doze It: Can you see underground?

Justin's father: Of course not!

E-Z Doze It: Well, neither can I. If I could, I wouldn't be pumping shit for a living.

Then the E-Z Doze It Man quotes Whitman:

> Whoever degrades another degrades me,
> And whatever is done or said returns at last to me.

That's how some stories end on this trip, the way I wish they would end.

My Mother Meets Van Gogh, Heidegger, and Derrida

The clouds above Blackfish Creek swirl in a spiraling dark vortex, and yet the sun stabs through, illuminating the Cherrystone Gallery across the road, blinding me with glare. At an opening one evening, an elderly man wearing an ascot and cape referred to the current show as overly derivative of Van *Goff.* A few minutes later, everyone pronounced the name as he had, and the front room, the back room, and the little garden, all resounded with gutturals, like a ward of patients clearing their throats.

My parents took me to a museum only once, to the Guggenheim's exhibit of Van Gogh when I was twelve. I hadn't seen much art, and neither had my mother, a graduate of Newtown High School in Queens whose most famous alumnus is Don Rickles. My father didn't finish eighth grade and the only art he saw was his father's forgeries and the work customers brought into the frame shop.

Two paintings from that show have stayed with me: *The Potato Eaters* and *Three Pairs of Shoes.* The shoes resembled my grandmother's high-topped black boots which my mother knelt before and laced up every morning after applying ointment to her mother's diabetes-ulcerated shins. And the potatoes resembled those she described baking with her friends in fires against the curbs of East Sixty-Second Street: charred on the outside, raw on the inside, and called "Mickeys," in honor of the Irish.

They are also memorable because my mother pointed out how poor the people were to have only potatoes for dinner, their faces so rough they looked like potatoes themselves. And the shoes, ravaged by labor. Unlike Heidegger, who said of *Three Pairs of Shoes,* "From the dark opening of the worn insides of the shoes the toilsome tread of the worker stares forth," and utterly unlike Derrida whose note on the same painting questioned what "constitutes a pair of shoes and how the elements of such combine different forms of reality," my mother said they showed how hard some people work.

THE ABORTION

During that year at SMU, Anne told me she thought she was pregnant. She told me in my office after class, sitting next to a poster of Farrah Fawcett, brought by a student who dared me to pin it up, and under a set of elk antlers from the previous occupant.

We couldn't understand how it happened, we had been careful, but something had gone wrong and now we faced the future surrounded by ridiculous walls in a diminished present.

Tests at Planned Parenthood proved positive. Anne made an appointment for the abortion and we dealt with the intervening days by drinking. Drinking and making love. We were becoming experts at oblivion and we erased the hours until the date.

Neither of us ever mentioned keeping the child, although once in the Lyons Pub I said, "Did you ever think that we, you know, we might ..."

"If we broke up, where would that leave us, and him. Or her," she said.

One morning, though, she didn't spring out of bed as usual, but lay on her side awhile, and I thought she'd been crying.

Ask me if what I have done is my life, William Stafford wrote. Roethke claimed in a notebook that poetry was more mysterious than sex. Roethke was wrong. Nature is supernatural.

I sat in the waiting room and watched her check in. I admired her composure that morning. She had asked if I thought this would bring us closer. We agreed it would, we hoped, we didn't know.

Anne returned a half hour later and said she wasn't pregnant after all. The test had been faulty. We were elated. It was only eleven a.m. but we got in the car and headed for the Tabu Lounge, a club owned by her friend.

We had committed to an abortion, but there would be no abortion.

There was a child we decided to keep from existing, but the child preempted our action and disappeared.

No life at all, it turned out, had been extinguished.

Yet something was extinguished, something had disappeared, whatever you want to call it, whatever you want to name it, whatever you want to call it, name it, call it.

ALMOST

After a few drinks, Anne reminded me that we hadn't used any protection during the previous week, and she may have gotten pregnant as recently as the night before.

Would there be a brother or sister of that child who did not exist?

No, that person would not exist and, eventually, neither would we.

Everybody Wants to Get into the Act

Anne tells me her watercolors have been selling well at a Dallas gallery and winning national prizes. She says she might want to try her hand at writing reviews. I tell her she's in the right place. Almost everyone on the Outer Cape is an artist, and the rest are art critics. A recent piece in the *New York Times* discussing Provincetown's bifurcated tax system reported one year-rounder's occupation as "part-time art critic." Who isn't? Even snowplow drivers have expressed their opinion of the Broken Arrow Gallery on Route 6, with its display windows full of orange-red sunsets and white lighthouses, by crashing into its mailbox and leaving it by the side of the road in two pieces: *Broken* and *Arrow.*

I ran into my son's former babysitter at the Stop & Shop, after having received a postcard from a gallery advertising her upcoming show.

"Congratulations, Regina," I said. "I didn't know you were an artist."

She leaned over the handle of her shopping cart, and said, very wearily, "Neither did I."

This is good and bad. Art lets people discover themselves, but also fool themselves. It doesn't matter whether their art is praised or reviled. They do it for the intoxication of the endeavor, to add a touch of rouge to a drab routine.

Which is why I created him.

THE DISCO DUCK

I took Anne to this bar in Wellfleet in 1979, the prime days of disco. Now it is called The Inn at Duck Creeke. Commercial fishermen drink here on weekend nights. Some are old salts with gray beards who serve as selectmen, their groomed hair bearing the flowing tracks of wide-toothed combs. Others are young men who "don't want to be chained to a desk," as one said to me. A woman named Nina arrives on "Studio 54 Saturdays" when the disc jockey plays music from that era and she stays till closing. She sits alone at the bar, wearing a tiny skirt, and steps onto the deck for a cigarette every fifteen minutes, followed by men who smoke as well as those who don't. After midnight, the dancing heats up, the music goes faster and faster, and soon every patron is on the floor and only Nina stays behind, refusing to dance when asked over and over by men and women. She is a sore spot with the DJ who motions to her, for her, imploring her to rise and step onto the parquet, but she just smiles and sips her mojito, looking at Wellfleet Harbor and the floodlights aimed at docked draggers and party boats. A car parked at the foot of the wharf has a large board leaning against its windshield that says, in dripping blood-red letters, *THE OYSTER THEIF MUST DIE.* The sign has authority, and the fact that its author did not know the "i before e rule" gives it even more power. Everyone wants to dance with Nina, who arrives and leaves alone. Until one night. The night Squeaky sat next to her.

Squeaky, captain of *The Sea Word,* known for his high-pitched voice and cordial manners, has one leg and walks with a crutch. He's held in esteem for his pronouncements, such as looking over the pool table and saying, "Remember—angle of incidence equals angle of refraction," and when a shot is especially difficult, he advises, "Ontogeny recapitulates phylogeny." Should a fight occur, he is the voice of reason. An altercation between a septic guy and an oil delivery man ended when he commanded, "Don't break up the *scene!*" He calmed a man who had been whacked on the skull with a beer bottle that did not break by buying him a drink, putting his arm around him, and providing simple counsel: "Get past the pain."

Nina left with him one night, and since then returns with him each Saturday. It's been months now. She's found the perfect mate. She doesn't dance and he can't dance. Although a Duck Creeke veteran recalled Squeaky on the parquet one time, only once, when he and his crew came upon an exaltation of tuna worth $50,000 on the Japanese market. The old timer said the one-legged man danced better than most men with two.

S

At seven a.m., Mrs. Post knocked on the door of our motel room at the Bull Ring. There was a phone call for Anne from her father. Her mother, ill with cancer, had taken a bad turn. She had to fly home immediately.

The morning was a panic of making reservations on the Provincetown plane to Boston, and then connections to Dallas. Packing and figuring out money, and her trying to eat the oatmeal Mrs. Post delivered to fortify her for the trip.

I paced around the room while she showered. I walked out on the deck. I hated to see her suffer the loss, I knew she loved her mother.

Mr. Post called a cab and then Anne was gone.

A rope rug, three aluminum chairs at a metal table with a frosted glass top. I separated the two single beds and made them up, washed the few glasses, and looked around to see if she had forgotten anything.

I liked the fragrance in the bathroom: her shampoo, toothpaste, tiny bar of motel soap surrounded by bubbles. And I liked remembering how she looked at me when she brushed her teeth as if I were the mirror, the way she grabbed the motel's can of cheap deodorizer and made a brisk S in the air....

Dress as Your Favorite Tree

At a panel discussion about post-modernist houses at the Wellfleet library, Walter Gropius's daughter, Ati, eighty, spoke about her father's success as director of the Bauhaus. She was asked how her father managed to keep harmony among that faculty, considering its distinctive personalities, including Paul Klee, Wassily Kandinsky and Johannes Itten, member of a fire cult. She said it was simple: whenever there was a fight over policy or practice, her father canceled all classes and declared a three-day party. At the festivity's end, everyone forgave or forgot what they had been fighting over. She added that Gropius provided the same solution to academic strife at Black Mountain College where he hosted costume parties with different themes. "The best was *Dress as your favorite tree*," she said, "because it was impossible to stay angry at a person covered in branches and leaves."

Some in the audience had strong feelings against these post-modernist constructions in town because of their bold designs and use of salvaged as well as cheap material such as Homasote, derived from recycled paper. At the question and answer period, a resident rose from his seat and called the structures monstrosities. He vehemently objected to Wellfleet's plan to honor them as historical sites. He was countered by a selectman who noted that the complainant had no credentials as an architectural critic. The man said that the town would soon be apprised of his credentials because the best form of architectural criticism is arson.

RUBBING SOUND

I brought my car to a mechanic in Provincetown because of a rubbing sound on the undercarriage. He found nothing wrong. The owner of the auto shop in Truro said it was coming from the front axle, a job too big for him. He recommended this place in Wellfleet where I've stopped now to get gas. The mechanic here said the problem was the rear axle and I should take it to the dealer in Orleans because it was a complicated repair. The dealer fixed the problem, which was with the exhaust system.

While I'm fueling up, I stare at the sky and a chickadee goes by with a twig in its beak. The night before I saw two flies on top of each other on the screen door, so it is truly the season of the birds and the bees.

I pay for the gas in the office and see the headline of the *Advocate*, which announces Nina was elected selectman in Wellfleet. In an interview before the election, she touted her qualifications for the post: she had inherited her house and never had a mortgage; therefore, she could sympathize with those who pay monthly bills. She had a trust fund and had never been in debt; therefore, she could serve as a model to help the town do the same.

Anne is wiping the windshield with a squeegee, her back to me, leaning across the hood to reach the middle of the glass. I recall our flight out here so long ago. She had the window seat, and I was in the middle. She had to use the bathroom which meant slipping by the snoring passenger on the aisle. She tried and tried, but he was slumped forward until he woke to this same view, close up.

"You know," I say to my father, "she looks almost exactly the same, after all these years."

"That reminds me," my father says. "Do you keep a fan belt in the trunk, like I told you? You should always have an extra fan belt."

"What does that have to do with anything?"

"You're in a gas station!"

"I wouldn't know how to put it on," I say.

69

"Someone will know. They might not have one, but they'll know."

"I was talking about Anne."

"I know you were."

"Then why did you change the subject?"

"Because she doesn't matter. Eventually, she'll disappear. That's what I know now. Ask me what difference the greatest love or hate has made."

CHRIST STOPPED AT EASTHAM

The title of Carlo Levi's novel, *Christ Stopped at Eboli,* means that the land south of Eboli, Italy, not visited by the redeemer, remained unsaved, and so was given over to heathens and chaos. The Cape Cod version is *Christ Stopped at Eastham,* the staid town that leads to the increasingly eccentric towns of Wellfleet, Truro, and Provincetown, each progressively crazier until travelers reach land's end and just leap into the sea. Some emerge as mermaids or mermen; others find a school to swim off with and are never seen again; some walk up and down the breakwater that leads to the Long Point Lighthouse; and a few settle in Hell Town until they die and join the ghosts of prostitutes, thieves, and murderers. Most become residents, making up the population.

Houses in Provincetown that have been floated over from Long Point bear bright blue plaques with a white line drawing of a house floating on waves. Stanley Kunitz lived in one of these relocated structures, delivered intact, furniture and all. He found a wad of bills between the mattress and the bedframe, which he claimed was the stash of a prostitute.

I'm traveling now through the dull stretch of Eastham, on the lookout for the descendants of Charon, the Eastham police who ticket everyone driving over forty mph, charging a fee for carrying us between the bourgeoisie and the underworld.

Eastham has three donut shops on a four-corner intersection at Brackett Road and Route 6—Dunkin' Donuts, The Hole in One, and Fleming's. At the Hole in One, a large coffee is called a Travel. Locals sit at a counter and banter with the staff who wait on a line that goes out the door. When it is my turn, the woman who will serve me looks over my shoulder, sees two regular customers enter, turns her back, fills their orders telepathically, and they slide to my right, plunking down exact change and leaving. I ask for two Travels and a glazed cruller which is a weighty six inches long. There is a riddle on the chalkboard over the coffee urns:

71

Q: Year-rounders have it. Summer people need it. If you eat it you die. What is it?

I grab my order, approach my car, and see two bumper stickers: *I'm Not On Your Vacation* and *I Support the War on Tourism.* A man in a camouflage outfit comes up to me and shows a fifty-dollar bill. He says he'll take two twenties for the fifty because he needs change right away to pay someone in a car farther down the lot. I say no thanks. Anne says go ahead. I say again, sorry.

As we're driving off, Anne presses me on why I walked away. "The ten dollars would have paid for our coffees," she says.

"It was probably counterfeit," I say.

"Maybe," she says, thinking it over.

"Besides," I say, "it would have been dishonest of me to take a fifty for two twenties, and my dishonesty would have made me a victim of his scam. Like my father told me when I was a kid, 'You can't cheat an honest man.'"

"That's right," my father says. "You can't."

"That's the title of a W. C. Fields movie," she says.

"Can't be!" I say.

"I'm positive. Fields runs a circus."

My father says, "Who cares where it comes from as long as it makes sense."

That was true. It did make sense. Still, I thought he had come by this tidbit of advice through experience, or maybe through *The Wandering Jew.* Now I'm recalling a Thanksgiving dinner where my father and uncles discussed our congressman sponsoring a boy from our parish to West Point in exchange for a donation from the Knights of Columbus.

An uncle said, "One hand washes the other," and everyone agreed.

There was a pause, then my father added, "And both hands wash the face."

All heads nodded again. I was impressed but wondered what was "the face?" Did each party belong to a larger, more powerful body that received fealty from both? I thought of his kicker to the old saying every time I heard it, mulling it without conclusion, feeling dumb, too dumb to ask about it.

Then one night, watching *The Honeymooners,* I heard Ralph Kramden say to Ed Norton, "One hand washes the other," and give a knowing look. Ed added, "And both hands wash the face!" It was Ed trying to keep up with Ralph in the wisdom department. In other words, it was meaningless.

My father's ethical training came from W. C. Fields and Jackie Gleason.

"Who cares where it comes from," my father says again.

Anne and I sip our Travels.

She figures out the answer to the donut shop's riddle: *Nothing.*

DEATH AND FAME

Budd Hopkins, member of the Abstract Expressionist group of painters, became so interested in alien-abduction phenomena, writing books on the subject and speaking at conferences, that his obituary in the *New York Times* noted that this second career "eclipsed the first." James Carroll escaped his earlier vocation as a priest when he won the National Book Award for his memoir, and said in his acceptance speech, "Now maybe the first line of my obituary won't read, 'James Carroll, ex-priest....'" Damien, the man who devoted his life to working with lepers on the island of Molokai, was remembered by Tomas Tranströmer:

> *Damien, for love, chose life and oblivion. He found death and fame.*

THE STORY OF BOB SHORTALL

Arnold's Lobster and Clam Bar, celebrated for its fried seafood, onion rings and "'50s Burgers," is also known for being owned by staunch Republicans. When Scott Brown ran against Elizabeth Warren for the Senate, the restaurant flew an enormous flag with his name on it. All of my liberal friends, myself included, said the same thing—they would never enter Arnold's again. This was our liberal response and it had the usual liberal effect: none. We couldn't hurt Arnold's by not patronizing it because we never patronized it in the first place.

I mention Arnold's because my childhood friend from New York, Bob Shortall, stopped there once. Why is it important? Because he was taking a trip to Provincetown, but never arrived. Like Christ, Bob stopped at Eastham, avoiding the very territory he had told me on the phone he was curious to see—gay culture, the bohemian climate, the street fare of female impersonators, drag queens, celebrity look-a-likes, puppeteers, and vendors of fancy cupcakes. Something stopped him in his tracks as he had been stopped in his tracks before. He blamed it on indigestion from the '50s Burger and went home. But I was not surprised. He had turned back previously in his life, and not just from geographical destinations. When Bob and I worked together with other teenagers at Paramount Pictures in Times Square, who were beginning to acquire a taste for coffee at break time, Bob continued sipping chocolate milk through a straw, looking up at us, eyebrows arched, as he hunched over his desk. After work, at the Terminal Bar, he ordered Coke while we drank beer and moved to bourbon. And as for that other bittersweet pleasure—sex—here, too, Bob abstained, and that is perhaps what made him change direction and head back to the city, away from the heat he must have felt coming from our Sodom and Gomorrah, and so he stopped at Eastham, bearing what Primo Levi called the manifest stigma of a protracted virginity.

A LIE

Anne says, "I let you get away with lying that you ran into me by accident on the stairwell at SMU when you really had it planned."

"I'm glad you did," I say. "Because today they call it stalking."

"I remember waiting to see if you'd tell me."

"I did!"

"Eventually."

"Who again snitched that I asked the secretary for your class schedule?"

"Professor Karp overheard you ask Peggy. He couldn't wait to let me know. Remember him, he wanted to get in my pants?"

"Now I remember. He taught Victorian novel and cut himself shaving almost every day, bits of tissue all over his neck."

"Gross!"

"I didn't know you knew. At least I was honest."

"I didn't mind. I already liked you."

"And I don't nick my throat while shaving."

"You're waiting to do it all at once!"

"If I do, I'll do it like I do everything these days. Theoretically."

FORT HILL

I had dinner here at a summer home made mostly of glass and overlooking Nauset Inlet. There were two couples and me. The owners discussed buying the condominium adjoining theirs on the Boston waterfront to better showcase their art, as the glass walls here limited the display area. The other had recently inherited a diamond mine in South Africa. Both talked of trips to a special town in the south of France whose name I could not understand, where they had stayed at the same bed-and-breakfast, sleeping on linens that aired on the line, dining on freshly baked brioche, vegetables grown in the garden, trout from the lake, and meat from beasts that roamed the fields. They were discussing the pottery sold in a nearby town when one of the women realized I was left out, and then said, "For John's sake, let me explain exactly what this place is...."

I only realize now, as I am driving near their house, that as much as I like these people ... my thoughts are interrupted by the comforting smell of burning leaves wafting through the air, something I also like. I drive a little farther and the aroma grows stronger though I must have long passed the diligent gardener and his bonfire.

My mother raked and burned leaves at our short-lived residence in Connecticut, happily surrounded by the swirling air, thrilled to simply have a yard. As I'm thinking of her, smoke rises from my engine! I pull over and open the hood and see the fiberglass lining charred and fuming. By the radiator, a squirrel's nest of leaves and twigs smolders. I dislodge it with a branch and go on my way. At Brownie's Texaco in Orleans, Mr. Brown checks the wires and belts and says no mechanical damage has been done. He advises that I fill a sock with mothballs and tie it near the washer fluid bottle to keep out the squirrels.

I drive away, possessed of an echo, but not a fate.

MONSTER FACE

My wife, my son, and I stopped at Bradlees department store years back, on our return trip from Boston, where Harry had undergone tests for a possible brain tumor at Children's Hospital. The procedure required he be asleep while his brain was monitored, so we had to keep him awake the night before, prodding and amusing him so he'd be unconscious when all the electrodes were attached to his head in the lab.

I told Harry to pick out a toy, and he spotted a large plastic skull called a Monster Face. The surface was perforated by rows of stitches, drops of blood, and half of a knife entering the temple. He held the enormous box, excited, maybe because it reminded him of his own skull, so probed and fixed with attachments that day. When he saw the price: forty-two dollars, he put it back on the shelf, and said, "For a minute, I thought I was going to get a Monster Face."

I didn't have to analyze that sentence then the way I'm doing now—it contains time, a mental process, the future, and an object of desire—to immediately take it to the cashier.

I hope I can find a place on this trip to use that line again, but if not, allow me to repeat it: "For a minute, I thought I was going to get a Monster Face."

Another Round

She was happiest when someone was buying her a drink, and I was happiest buying one for her. Waiting at The Jersey Lily ("I always arrived first. It was my lot to wait for her," as Rousseau said), I examined her entrance, that quick stride that moved her shoulders side to side like someone doing exercises to grow stronger, not to repair damage. A voice at the bar called to her, "I'm in love!" to which she replied, "No, you're not!" without looking her admirer's way, and sat down across from me, irradiating the dark booth.

That night she talked about her favorite class, Women's Studies, and the teacher, Dawn Parcell, who discussed her career in academia and the obstacles she faced as a female. Dawn also spoke personally about her marriage to the manager of a bluegrass band, a man often on the road, but always in close and intimate touch. Anne wanted a relationship like the one Dawn described: independent careers, perfectly and happily matched.

As Anne continued describing Dawn, I was watching Dawn's husband, Jim, over Anne's shoulder. I recognized him from a department party. He sat at the bar with a woman. At one point, he lifted a large white box from the foot rail and gave it to her. I told Anne who turned to see the woman unfold a fur jacket from the tissue.

"Well," Anne said, and she flushed. "I feel sorry for Dawn. She seems so happy, so reasonable about everything, as if she has it all figured out."

"Looked at from the height of reason, life seems like a grave disease, and the world like a madhouse."

"Let's not be reasonable then."

"Another round?"

My League

The Orleans Firebirds play in Eldredge Park on Route 28, part of the Cape Cod Baseball League.

In my league, there are foul lines, yes, but there are places where the white chalk has completely faded. And there are foul poles, but they have been pushed so far left and right that everything is fair. The stands and the diamond have merged. Athletes and fans intermingle.

This is the best feature of my league—those from antiquity, both hall of famers and utility players, take the field.

The only thing that remains traditional, eternal, and everlasting is that there is no clock, and any game can go into extra innings, and that's where we are now, with no end in sight.

My Way

"I see you're wearing my pinkie ring," my father says.

"Yes, I got it sized."

He's referring to the thick gold ring with an orange carnelian carved with two figures: Venus holding a platter over the head of a dancing cupid. He wore it all his life and gave it to me as a present in our Queens living room during cocktail hour the day before I left for my first teaching job at SMU.

"I thought you lost it."

"No, though I almost did."

"I know, you told me."

I was with Anne and another couple at a restaurant after seeing *Manhattan,* drinking heavily as usual. My friend and I were taking turns tossing the heads of flowers from the table's bouquet into the cleavage of our dates. When we ran out of blossoms, I lobbed my ring which landed on the rug's orange/brown geometric pattern, and I was in a panic under the table, afraid I wouldn't find it.

"You were careless when you were young," my father says. "You didn't give a damn about most things. Your friends and girlfriends were like that too."

"By things, you mean money?"

"Money. Your appearance. A job."

I have to agree. I remember telling Anne, "Rules are for those who follow them," as I ushered students into a university ballroom where alcohol was served, a small infraction, but significant at the time. Anne was not careless so much as carefree, a wealth-infused independence. We arrived at our state of indifference by different routes.

"I don't have any regrets," I say.

"When someone says that, I know they have regrets or they wouldn't have brought it up," my father says.

"Why throw a wet blanket on this trip? I'm trying to have some fun in the little time we have left," I tell him.

"You have a strange idea of fun."

"You should talk. I mean after the stunts you told me you pulled in the navy."

"You've never been cooped up on a ship!"

The prank I remember best involved the doctor on his aircraft carrier who was also a devout minister. Before the men went on shore leave, he gave speeches on temperance and self-control. After a three-day binge in Barcelona, my father made an appointment to see him, on a bet with his shipmate, to complain about a lump in his penis. The doctor listened to my father, inhospitable, unsympathetic, and finally shocked when he pulled back my father's foreskin to find a piece of popcorn.

"I guess you had to do something for laughs," I say.

"Now that I think of it, that doctor did say something that day I remember. I put it in my notebook: *Each bug dies in its own way.*

THE MONUMENT

A boy on a sled collided with a tree here, at the bottom of this deep incline, and died of head trauma. The town, in memoriam, razed the oak and built a stone monument in its place. The next year a boy, also sledding, crashed into the monument and he, too, was killed.

THE HEYDAY OF PIRACY

The car in front of me has a ZooQuarium bumper sticker. A few weeks ago, I wondered if this tourist attraction in West Yarmouth had closed so I checked it out on the web. Half the posts said it was boarded up and the other half said it's open. It seems there is little difference.

The reviews:

"Most of the advertised animals were nowhere to be found. Many empty cages. The bird show is not much of a show. A kestrel flew several times past our ears, a red-tailed hawk sat on the guide's arm while she walked back and forth talking, and three seagulls picked at their feet in the background. That was the show."

"Totally disappointing touch tank—there was nothing in it and the water was all brown."

"As far as the seals—last time I went the seals had recently passed away from some disease, and they haven't replaced them yet."

And one complaint had a theme:

"The fact sheet overemphasized the digestive tract:

* *Llamas have a communal poop pile.*
* *Sea lions' poop is very greasy because they eat a lot of fish.*
* *A mouse's skeletal structure can be re-created from an owl's vomit because owls don't digest bones.*"

And finally:

"They opened the door as I approached, and I said, 'Hi, I just called. We drove forty-five minutes ...' Then I was interrupted by a man named Lou who told me to 'get here on f@*king time.' I was shocked and asked him if I heard him right. Another employee named Nancy told me that they just had someone call and swear at them. I told them I just had called but didn't swear. The woman who answered the phone assured Lou and Nancy that the person who called had a raspy voice, which I do not, and that the person WASN'T ME. This didn't stop Lou from being rude. I was shocked to find out that Louis Leed, the guy who swore at me in front of a bunch of children, was the owner. I had this conversation in front of my fifteen-month-old daughter and wife. I WILL NEVER GO BACK and I implore that others don't either."

Cape Cod Times Update: December 2015
Local officials are looking forward to the redevelopment of a prime property that has been abandoned for the past three years.

Barry Clifford finalized the purchase of the sprawling ZooQuarium. The explorer who discovered the three-hundred-year-old pirate ship, *Whydah,* will open a museum offering a close-up look at the booty Captain "Black Sam" Bellamy amassed before the ship went down off the Wellfleet coast.

"The pirate museum is a wonderful addition to Yarmouth and it will continue the tradition of family-friendly entertainment at the site," wrote Yarmouth's community development director.

Tanks in the metal building have been removed so its high ceilings can accommodate Clifford's scale model of the *Whydah,* which stands thirty feet tall.

Much of the exhibit will feature items never shown on the Cape before, Clifford said. One of those highlights is the ship's oven.

The plan also calls for a laboratory where the public can watch archaeological experts extract coins, jewelry, and even human bones from hardened chunks of sand and ocean debris.

The pool where marine performers entertained crowds in the past will be replaced with a stage where speakers spin yarns about the heyday of piracy.

THE FIREBOAT

Snow's Home and Garden, the largest independent store on Cape Cod, has an *Upstairs, Downstairs* atmosphere. The Snow family has managed it through four generations. Weathervanes line the shelves along with nautically themed serving bowls, teak furniture, stationery, and hand-carved whales and sea serpents. They sell silver cocktail shakers and one-ounce atomizers for spraying vermouth across the top of a Martini. The staff is trained to be accommodating, but they have the feel of butlers both obsequious and imperious. When you ask for help finding an item, most salespeople will nod, turn their backs, and expect you to follow.

One day, waiting on the checkout line, I heard a small boy crying, very loudly. It was an agonizing call, with words I couldn't understand. His screams came closer and closer until he passed right in front of me: a four-year-old carried over his father's shoulder as he yelled the sentence that finally became clear, "I want that fireboat!" Then he caught his breath and yelled again, "I want that fireboat!"

I could picture it: red and white, bright lights flashing above the cabin, and a little hose on deck that can be wound and unwound.

"I want that fireboat!"

The check-out people looked annoyed, unsympathetic because he was disturbing the very soul of Snow's. I wanted that fireboat myself. I wanted to give the child that fireboat. What could the fireboat have meant to him? What fires at sea would it extinguish with him as captain? And without a captain, what fires will continue to burn?

The Mayflower Assisted-Living Center

"I hate to tell you, Dad, but we're approaching the Mayflower in Yarmouth."

"Keep going!" he says.

When my mother's dementia worsened, and my father had a stroke that left him using a walker, I sold their apartment in Boston and found an assisted-living center on the Cape. Admission to the Mayflower required an interview to prove they were intellectually competent.

The director and head nurse sat behind a desk and faced my parents: my mother, always cheerful even when disoriented; my father, alert and active, reading the *Wall Street Journal* every day and buying and selling stocks. He worried that his eighth-grade education would hinder him. I worried that my mother would fail. My mother was not worried at all. She was out of her mind.

They asked my father to name the year. He was nervous and got it wrong several times but finally gave the right answer. He knew his birthday and the day of the week.

It was my mother's turn—she was smiling and happily looking from face to face.

The nurse asked her the year. Correct. The month. Correct again. The date and the day. Perfect. My father and I were amazed and the administrators satisfied. The director complimented my mother on her sharp mind and lively personality. They were delighted to have a new couple pay their tremendous rates, and the nurse shook their hands and welcomed them, especially my mother.

My mother smiled and said to the director, "You might want to know something."

We waited.

"There's a calendar right behind your desk!" All eyes focused there, on the large numbers in big squares, but the director and nurse took this as evidence of my mother's acuity and wit. It was the latter; she had retained that, and my parents moved in with no trouble, but they would eventually leave in a tragic way due to my mother's failed mind.

"They should have asked us to name the date we die," my father says. "Every year we pass it. That would be a real test."

HERE AND THERE

The nutty, marginal stations broadcast at the far end of the radio dial, and today I've tuned in a Catholic priest who says it doesn't matter where you're buried because, at the end of the world, all bodies will rise from the dead, healthy and whole.

I imagine my mother's memories gathering together, pinned back into her brain, the resurrection of her mind as well as her body. And my father's regrets about wishing he knew earlier what he knew at his death, all those disappointments wiped away.

My daydream continues as the priest continues, saying that the fight over Bishop Fulton Sheen's body, now at Saint Patrick's Cathedral, but sought by the Illinois parish of his birth, is pointless. He condemns the compromise that happened to Saint Catherine: her head in Siena, her trunk in Rome. He says the resurrection of the body makes futile the pact that put Saint Francis Xavier's right arm in Italy and the rest of him in India.

What about someone driving one road, his heart on another?

THE MENSCH TAX

Anne and I were introverts masquerading as extroverts. We went along with the crowd, sometimes led the crowd, high-spirited and convivial, and yet we retreated into ourselves when alone and walked the black dog. A friend mentioned that Anne was paying the "mensch tax," the tax levied for never showing a vulnerability, for putting up a strong front so that no one thinks of you as being in need, so you are never the recipient of kind words or gestures or even a professional boost because you have pretended you need nothing. When two people like that meet, they need each other.

A Sick Goose

"Why didn't you stick with painting after you graduated?" I ask Anne. "I remember how much you loved art. Why law?"

"I had to look out for myself, that's why. My mother had died, my father was drinking. It was the practical thing to do."

"I was never practical," I say.

"Easy for a man," she says. "Every job offer was stupid, like being a TV weathergirl. Besides, I'd never been around painters. I never heard anyone say, 'I'm a painter.' It seemed impossible."

"You've done pretty well."

"More with law," she says. "I still don't call myself an artist. When I say that, I feel weird."

"I know what you mean. I read somewhere that just as everyone has a brain, a heart, and a spleen, they also have art in their bodies. And if you develop that part out of proportion to the other parts, it can be embarrassing."

"Like an overfed goose with a fat liver," she says.

"Yes, like that, but the liver tastes great."

"Because the goose is sick!"

AND NOW YOU'RE UP TO DATE

Anne wants to change the radio station from WFCC, Cape Classical, where the hosts pronounce the names of Italian composers with a singsong lilt. I ask her to wait for the news at the top of the hour because I think she'll enjoy it, and here it comes, two simple stories given in ninety seconds:

Workers were removing trees at a residence on Freeboard Lane, when a neighbor reportedly stormed out of her house, ordering them to stop, went back inside, and returned to the scene armed with several eggs.

Witnesses recount the enraged female launching eggs at the workers' van.

There were shells stuck to the van, some on the roadway, broken yolks, whites dripping from a chrome bumper.

Police arrived, knocked repeatedly, but were unable to get the suspect to come to the door.

The tree workers had to hustle, leery about the possibility of incoming eggs.

Police stood by until the men were able to finish their day's work and safely leave the hostile surroundings.

A malfunctioning wall outlet ignited a chair in an East Dennis home yesterday. Firefighters arrived at 97 Anchor Lane at 3:02 a.m. to find all occupants outside and a chair in a front bedroom on fire. Firefighters removed the chair and a blanket that had been folded on it and quickly extinguished the flames.

After this story, the announcer says, "And now you're up to date!" I give Anne the go-ahead to switch stations and she lands on 1010 WINS, New York City's all-news station. The first words we hear are, "The severed head tested positive for AIDS."

THE MOCKINGBIRD

Our days in Dallas found us attending an exhibition of Venus flytraps at the botanical gardens; a lecture by Darius Milhaud's widow; the back door of Gina's bakery for warm bread after the bars closed; a concert by Zorro and the Blue Footballs; and the concrete porch of my garden apartment at three a.m. listening to the rambunctious sounds of my favorite bird, the mockingbird, an amusement fueled by brandy.

Inside my furnished rooms, Anne had a way of turning pages so that it became a boisterous, physical act. Her eyes seemed to ignite the print, her hand to fan the flame. I admired her concentration, going from page to page of *Pride and Prejudice,* burning through it, her profile so reserved in contrast to her tomboyish manhandling of the book. The placid face, the darting eyes and the quick hands created a tension that was palpable, almost unbearable and I couldn't help but interrupt. She smiled and shook me off. So I'd flip through my own book, usually poetry, which I would read and stop and look up and pretend to consider....

In company, I'd catch her looking at me, predicting my response to a remark, which had me looking to her in the same way. Soul mates is too thrifty a description. A linkage of sensibilities in the Over-Soul too grandiose. Maybe the bumper sticker we saw that had us laughing comes close: *Two drifters off to see the world ...*

As a child, I pitied those kids who complained "Not fair!" during a game when a passing car knocked a ball awry and they demanded a "do-over." It seemed the cry of losers, the hopeless ones railing against the sky, the universe, the controlling gods. Why not admit I just said the phrase under my breath? It doesn't seem fair to be living that time again in mimicry, but perhaps all along I have preferred the mockingbird's rendition to the original.

SID AND NANCY COME TO CAPE COD

Willy's World Fitness Center in Eastham advertised, "Splash in our salt water pool" and on my first day there, someone did: a teenager drove his car through the huge plate-glass window and directly into the water.

Men under doctor's orders walked forlornly from one weight machine to another, carrying spray bottles and rags to wipe off the equipment. The only sounds on those mornings were grunting and straining. When a woman joined the club, the sole female, she was followed from exercise station to exercise station by many members, suddenly talkative, including the retired cartoonist and the retired entertainment impresario. Forced laughter could be heard now and then from the woman who wanted to get on with her workout.

Since it was close quarters, I overheard their stories. One had written a pamphlet on city noise, proposing that traffic cops replace whistles with kazoos. Another had managed Rosemary Clooney's career for thirty years. A refined, scholarly-looking man said that he had sold Sid Vicious the weapon with which he murdered his girlfriend, Nancy, in the Chelsea Hotel. This got my attention. I asked the receptionist about him and she told me that it was true. He had been a druggist who owned a pharmacy in Chelsea, and his inventory included scissors imported from Germany, a pair of which Sid bought, used in the stabbing, and which were traced to his shop after the murder.

THE ALCHEMIST

Here is the dilapidated residence of Dr. Anthony Galante, who retired from teaching chemistry at Nauset Regional High School to work on his experiments to turn one thing into another, with the goal of getting rich.

He fails, year after year, to turn foil into silver, water into fuel, fabric into armor—he came close with the latter but learned a Seattle company had already invented a "tin cloth" shirt. His house has fallen down around him from neglect, the lawn alternately overgrown and barren, emerald-colored moss clogging the gutters, and grass somehow growing on the roof. He has succeeded in transforming one thing: his home into a few corridors of mildewed sticks.

I ask myself about his alchemical drive: how is it different from any of us who try to turn the sweat of our labor into dollar bills?

Galante's ex-wife, known as the most beautiful woman to have graduated from Nauset High, left him because of his obsession. After a few drinks, someone near him at the bar will be sure to mention her, to which Galante sometimes replies, "Beautiful is as beautiful does," which made me conclude that beautiful did not do much, particularly in the way of lovemaking. She came into The Fairway years ago, and it was true; she was beautiful, tall and thin with large eyes. She did not take a stool but remained standing even when Galante put his arm around her waist and tried to guide her to a seat. She twisted quickly away, an exotic fish that flinched when you neared the glass.

I ran into him at Fanizzi's. He asked me within minutes if I had any interest in alchemy. Before I answered, I was interrupted by a roar from the patrons on the other side of me. They were discussing "the blue zone," the location of people who live past one hundred. Galante immediately leaned over and joined the conversation, saying it should be possible to change age into youth. When everyone laughed, he said that opposites are closely related, like sides of a coin. He asked his bar mates if they had any interest in alchemy. After they kidded him for a while, Galante told the story of a man who tried to change

95

coal to gold but got stumped at a certain point. Doing research on the Internet, he discovered that a wise woman, a recluse in Tibet, was said to hold the answer. He dropped everything to find her, and it took years. When he got to her remote village, and found her even more remote house, he knocked on the door. The wise woman in Tibet turned out to be the most beautiful woman in Tibet. He composed himself long enough to describe his experiment. She said she was busy, she was alone, her husband was on a trip and she had time for only one question and no more—he would get the answer to his single question and then he must leave. Galante said he understood the man's quest, that he himself had a single question that would mean everything to him. A barfly guessed, "When is your husband coming home?" Laughter drowned out the rest of the story, and it remains unfinished.

Galante left to have a cigarette and I watched him on the deck as he looked over the bay at the incoming tide. I saw everything through his eyes: tobacco into ash, evening turning to night, shore into sea, ice melting to water in the Jack Daniel's in front of me.

The barmaid, a summer hire from Croatia, spoke to me about the man in Galante's story in a thick accent. "He didn't want gold," she said. "He wanted women." I turned the conversation back to the blue zone and asked her if she would like to live to be one hundred. She said, "In your country, I would like to live to one hundred, but in my country, no."

She asked me if I would consider moving to a blue-zone country, like Greece or Japan. I told her I was in a zone from which I could not depart: the gray zone, where people teach until they are one hundred.

Galante did not manage to transform his age into youth. He died a year later, flesh into dust.

PEEPING PODRESCU

Anne reads aloud a story from the *Cape Codder:*

ORLEANS—A 29-year-old Bulgarian man whose visa to stay in the country expired in 2012 was sentenced Wednesday to 2½ years in the Barnstable County Correctional Facility for photographing a young girl showering inside a bathhouse at Nickerson State Park in July. Petru Podrescu also was found guilty of trespassing on state property. On July 6, Brewster police responded to a call from a park ranger about a suspicious vehicle. They were joined by a state police trooper when a report came in of a "peeping Tom" who had held a cell phone under the door of a shower videotaping a young girl, a juvenile, as she was showering. The girl noticed the camera and began screaming, and the perpetrator fled.

Police found Podrescu squatting against a tree, holding a bag containing fishnet stockings and a cell phone. They also found a considerable amount of worn underwear and bras in the trunk of his car.

In court, Podrescu admitted to videotaping the girl.

At the time, Podrescu was out on bail for attempting to run over a woman at Willy's World Fitness Center in North Eastham.

Permanent Halloween

Life-size vampires; witches stirring a pot; scrawny zombies with outstretched arms; white webbing in the tree branches: this front yard is permanently Halloween. For decades, the owners festooned their property on each holiday: sleighs, elves, and Santa Claus for Christmas; leprechauns on Saint Patrick's Day; six-foot-tall bunnies and egg-filled trees at Easter.

Cars stopped and families posed for photos on this magical stage.

One of the owners died on October 31 last year, and the set has frozen in time. Rumors say the survivor is still inside.

I took my parents here when my son was small. They were impressed but my mother wanted to show Harry an old-fashioned Halloween, the way it used to be. His friends came to our house and my mother led them in bobbing for apples. She blindfolded them and placed their hands into bowls of peeled grapes, cold oatmeal, and spaghetti in oil. She sent every kid home with a little sack of candy and trinkets which she had bought at Job Lots in New York.

The next day we were swamped with calls of complaint. The children were smoking fake cigarettes, each kid puffing away, practicing for the real thing. I looked into our son's bag and found an authentic-looking pack of Camels that said, "Just Like Dad," on the front. Each smoke had a simulated lit tip of red foil and powder inside.

One outraged parent showed up at our front door and confronted my mother about the destructive force of these exact replicas. My mother yelled back at the neighbor, defending the world where the real and the imaginary meet and each imbues the other with its opposite characteristic.

STRING THEORY

I often stop at Lox, Stock and Bagel for coffee; one morning the shop was closed. The next day I read in the paper that Lucinda, the owner, was taken to the Cape Cod Hospital emergency room after having almost choked to death on a piece of string cheese. The doctors removed a short segment from her nasal passage, but she insisted she inhaled a lengthier piece. A week later it was still the topic of her conversation. She went on about the size of the missing strand as I waited for the order of the portly man ahead of me to be filled—he had requested *twelve onion bagels, somewhat heavily buttered*—swearing she would solve the mystery, that it must be around somewhere.

I could picture that piece of string cheese as if it had a life of its own, on the counter, around the leg of a chair. It reminded me of my stay at Baptist Hospital in Nashville for brain surgery, a benign tumor. A cleaning woman washed the floor each day, and once a string broke off the mop and stuck to a corner. As I could hardly move, I felt a delirious connection to the stranded inch. The next day, she mopped the floor again, and I was sorry it would go, but later I saw it across the room. This went on all week—sloshed from one wall to another. The day I was released, I took it with me, and I have it here on my desk, a souvenir, a survivor, a fellow commuter.

MONKEY IN THE MIDDLE

The Parnassus Bookshop sells used books, new books by locals, and advanced review copies. When Anne and I were together, I bought the galley of a forthcoming anthology of personal essays by multiracial writers, signed by the editor. I thought it would be useful for the course she was taking: Multicultural Visions. The book had a ridiculous title, *Monkey in the Middle,* but was unread, in perfect shape. Anne liked the collection, so I later tried to get her a finished copy, in hardcover, with the dust jacket, but it turns out the publisher withdrew the book and it was never published.

My gift was a signed copy of a book that doesn't exist.

HEY

A thirty-foot-long flag flies day and night at Exit 6, marking the truck stop housing Burger King, Subway, Dunkin' Donuts, Mobil Mart, and unheated restrooms whose doors do not completely close. School children on class trips dance around those waiting for the buses to New York, Providence, Boston, or Foxwoods. A huge display of color brochures for whale watches and museum tours stands near a five-foot glass case housing a claw that dangles above a bin of stuffed animals. Its sign says *Play Till You Win*, which assumes infinite funds and timelessness. One night two boys of no more than twelve, stocky kids with shaved heads, played till they lost. One grabbed the machine, toppled it to the floor, and the other raised a metal chair high in the air, bringing it down and shattering the glass. During this assault, a voice half-heartedly yelled, "Hey!"

As they grabbed the toys, one boy said, "I thought it would be harder to break."

"Hey!"

In bad weather, I park in the commuter lot here and take the bus. Passengers wait in a kiosk of glass and steel, open at both ends. During rain and snow, everyone huddles in the middle.

Warner Rose, a retired police chief, sells tickets in his truck from two a.m. to nine a.m., accompanied by his pet, Max, a tiny burrowing owl who walks back and forth on the dashboard. Like me, Warner always tunes his radio to the Cape's classical station so that Mozart, Brahms and Bach pervade the air around him. A truly strong man, he wears a thin jacket or short-sleeve shirt in all seasons, only occasionally running his engine for warmth. I immediately recognized him as Hermes, god of travelers. He says his endurance evolved from years of directing traffic and other on-the-job outside activities.

I once said to him, "See those guys jumping a car's battery?"

He looked over at the raised hoods. "Supposedly," he said, adding, "a few hours ago two undertakers shifted a corpse from the back seat of one car to another." His mythological proportions also remind me of the Argus and, like Argus, Warner has a hundred eyes, and a hundred eyes are necessary to monitor the goings-on here.

I'm usually one of the commuters surrounding his truck as we wait for the bus. I tell the group that I came home late the other night after a storm and, as I raked snow off the passenger side of the car, I was startled by motion in the back seat of the vehicle next to me, where someone slept. Warner says a lot of people sleep in cars here and that homeless men and women camp on the hill that abuts the parking lot, sometimes wandering around and lifting untended bags from those going to the airport.

One of the men says, "Live and let live." He's a musician who dresses as John Philip Souza and tours with a marching band. He has suffered burns to his cheeks and neck from a childhood fire. We stand in the wind, and the colder we get the redder we get, but as his scar tissue becomes more pronounced, his face turns whiter and whiter.

"'Live and let live' is very close to 'Die and let die,'" Warner says.

I know each bus driver from my years of commuting. Michael drives so cautiously you might as well take the bus that arrives a half hour later because his bus and the next will pull into South Station simultaneously. Kelly is a hypochondriac and his voice booms through the microphone asking the forty-seven passengers for aspirin or cough drops. Once he described his chapped lips so vividly a woman rushed to his aid and then we heard her say, "No! No! Keep it!" Kelly looked particularly grim one morning as he took my ticket. I asked if he was okay. He whispered, "The inspector of the bus is on the bus."

All drivers, no matter their age or size, have the same dead-on gaze, an entrenched focus you see on horses pulling carriages around Central Park, incapable of a quick glance.

We are all strangers and yet we are intimates. Three classes are represented among the passengers: the upper crust, elderly riders on their way to medical appointments; the poor, some holding full black plastic trash bags; the middle class, like me, who discuss the weather and the time. We are the only class that talks. The rich and the poor are silent.

On the days I arrive after Warner has left, I buy tickets at the Mobil Mart from Tahoma, whose name, he said, means "with a cute personality."

I once gave into the temptation to buy a lottery ticket for a $100 million prize.

"You think you're going to win?" Tahoma asked.

He turned to the next in line, refusing to take my money.

Today, I drive into the lot and make Warner a present of a bottle of Old Crow because this is my last trip and I won't be seeing him again until fall. He shows the label to his owl who does not respond.

"What are your plans for the summer?" he asks.

"I've got a ton of books to read," I say.

"I don't know," he says. "Too much reading. You'll end up talking to yourself."

I drive off and kid my father, "That's what I have you for, so I don't have to talk to myself."

"Isn't talking to yourself what they call writing?" he says. "Why aren't you writing?"

John Skoyles

OUT OF THE INKWELL

Marshall from Marshall's Used Books calls and says the book I ordered on Jung's active imagination has arrived.

My father asks about it, and I say it's weird, that you focus on a poster, or a painting, until it comes to life, and a figure leaps out at you.

"It sounds like a cartoon from when I was a kid," he says. "The artist dipped his pen into a bottle of ink and drew a clown, Koko, who jumped off the page and into, I guess you'd call it, the real world."

And that's where I've brought my father. Until he returns to the inkwell.

The Heartbreak Hotel Meets Harvard Yard

I tell Anne that years ago my wife dropped Harry off at this Burger King and I picked him up on my way home from Boston. Harry and I drove to Lupo's Heartbreak Hotel in Providence to see Rancid, his favorite punk band. It was 1998 and he was twelve.

It was drizzling when we arrived and I felt out of place at Lupo's wearing my tan London Fog raincoat and carrying an umbrella. I ordered a Jack Daniel's, which was served in a plastic cup by a tattooed, pierced, and pink-haired woman in a tank top who put her fingers into the drink as she poured, so a dose of perfume gave the bourbon an added lilt. We stood in the front of the stage, the lights came on, and Rancid's skinny, very pale lead singer, yelled, "I figured out the problem Yea the problem is you didn't see us comin' Now there's nothin' you can do...." He was pointing at me. I told my son the singer seemed deathly white and Harry said his name was Lint.

The night before I had attended a reading by Seamus Heaney at Harvard, where he had returned for a visit after having taught at the college for years. Helen Vendler introduced Heaney as she stood at a podium emblazoned with the crimson Harvard fleur-de-lis, saying she couldn't believe it had been so long since Seamus had first arrived at Harvard and how long it's been since he left Harvard, and he thanked her and said he himself couldn't believe how long he had been at Harvard and how long he had been away from Harvard, so it was impossible to forget that they both were at or had been at Harvard—unlike us, who were simply guests of Harvard, a hotel without a heart.

LAST LAUGH

Did you hear that? Of course you didn't. It was my father. My pact with him was that he speaks only to me. But sometimes, if you concentrate very hard, you can feel the dead overhearing your thoughts. My father always said his favorite sound was a good laugh, particularly a girl's laugh, and he just heard it. Anne liked that last part about Harvard and the heart.

TWO FINCHES

Anne walked into my apartment on Mockingbird Lane on my birthday carrying a large cube wrapped in a towel. She removed the cover to present a cage containing two finches.

Percy, a Society finch, sang to Fanny, a Zebra finch and, as he sang, he swiveled and pivoted on the perch toward her. She responded to his cheery notes, moving her tail sideways, so he could mount her. For the rest of the day, she flew back and forth, honking through her bright orange beak.

A month later, I watched Fanny lay an egg, and she did so from a high perch, as there were no nesting materials. It hit the floor without breaking and Percy cocked one eye toward it, then raced down, rolled it into a corner, and sat on it. Fanny laid two more eggs, and they took turns roosting on them as best they could without a nest.

Anne and I went to the pet store where she bought the birds and explained the situation to the owner. He said they were able to mate but, because they were two different species, their infertile eggs would not hatch.

I said I hated to see them waiting like that, for something that would never happen.

The owner said, "What else do they have to do?"

IMMORTALITY

I suddenly remember I'm supposed to give a makeup test to a poetry student who was sick for the final exam.

I have it: I'll quote Ezra Pound, "A man can be made immortal with just six lines," and tell him, "For Tuesday, turn in six lines. Pass/fail."

No One

I gave the finches to my mother in New York, who loved birds. Fanny's honk sounded exactly like the lobby buzzer that came through the intercom to her apartment. With every honk, my mother rose from her chair, walked down the hall, and pressed the button, saying in a welcoming voice, "Hello? Who is it? Who's there?"

Dad and Old Granddad

Anne took me to her parents' mansion in the Turtle Creek section of Dallas when they were away on a cruise. Everything was grand. We drank Old Grand-Dad in a living room that was so huge I didn't notice the grand piano. I asked what her father did to earn $400,000 a year, while I was making $12,500.

We went into his study, a dark room with mahogany panels, and shelves displaying ships in bottles and duck decoys.

I stood at his enormous desk. On the green blotter was a stack of pages, five hundred or more, the contract between the Dallas Cowboys football team and Arlington Stadium.

"Different from your slim volume of modern verse," Anne didn't have to point out.

Rings

My son calls my cell to say he's getting married. I congratulate him. I love his girlfriend, Heather, and am happy for them both. When we hang up, I tell Anne the news and say the first words that come to my mind, from Philip Larkin:

> He married a woman to stop her getting away.
> Now she's there all day.

"Just like what Mrs. Post said to you," she says.

"Yes," I say. "Exactly like Mrs. Post. *Don't let her get away,* she said about you."

"Like quarry," Anne says.

I remind Anne that she almost didn't get away in Dallas. She had to move because her landlord was selling the complex and buying out all the leases. Anne found a house with an entire floor for rent and suggested we live together. The owner was an old woman who wanted a married couple for stability, so we bought wedding rings and an engagement ring at the costume jewelry counter of Dillard's.

Anne kept these on her dresser, for when we would see the place. I often opened the box, imagining being married and imagining pretending to be married. Soon after, her landlord wrote that the sale fell through and her lease would be honored after all.

The rings took on a different aura. They were there and not there. They were real and they were imaginary. They were bits of costume jewelry—costumes without an occasion. I put mine on one night when she was in the shower just to see what it felt like. I was staring at the back of my hand when a dog barked in the distance and every so often a voice called its name.

A Little Drinking Village with a Fishing Problem

Chatham is not a literary town, and it's the only town on the Cape that votes Republican, so I was surprised when my friend from college, Tracy Kidder, a Pulitzer-prize-winning writer, called me to say he was in a bookstore there to promote a new book. He remarked on the white picket fences surrounding every house and felt the town was populated by retired dentists.

He got a kick out of the highly rhetorical shop names: he bought a sandwich from The Pampered Palette and a bottle of wine at The Epicurean Wine Cellar. Afterward, on Main Street, he passed Ducks in the Window, which sold nothing but little rubber ducks.

When he arrived at the bookstore, a huge poster for Tracy's appearance announced, "She will be reading from her new book at four p.m."

ASHES TO ASHES

Sandwich is celebrated for its glass museum and working grist mill in the center of town, but it was not appreciated by Thoreau, who found it "half a Sandwich at most, and that must have fallen on the buttered side." A plaque honors the whaler Peleg Nye, born here in 1817 and famous for being knocked off his ship and down the throat of a sperm whale, which spat him out alive. The library offers a lecture series that includes a talk titled, "What Do Dolphins Mean in Dreams?"

I always feel cheered when I glance at the mill where people surround the pond feeding waterfowl, others carrying sacks of freshly ground corn. My dyslexic nephew sent a postcard to me from here, writing that he "fed dread to the bucks." It turns out he was prescient, the ducks are fed dread, not by visitors, but by a snapping turtle who makes his home here, and who sends tourists away wondering why, when a mother duck glides across the pond with her ducklings, every so often one of them disappears, suddenly yanked beneath the surface.

The Sandwich Harbor holds the ashes of my mother and father. I poured their remains off the pier of this town they lived near in their last years. I park there now, and stare at the whitecaps. My parents have dissolved into the blue, massive harbor. Out of the froth, their figures rise up, and I remember flying with Anne to Queens to introduce them to her, who has already left the car, searching for a path through beach grass where we can take an extended walk that I will pretend to enjoy.

She played the guitar for them after dinner, using my old acoustic instrument from childhood, given to me so I could take lessons on the public television station. The program was *Folk Guitar with Laura Weber*, whom I just Googled and see she died on the same date as I'm writing this, in 1995, when she was seventy! Hello, Laura! If I still had my guitar, I would play "Streets of Laredo" for you!

Anne left my parents' living room early to read in bed. My mother called this "very sophisticated," but resented it. When I was alone with my parents, I praised Anne's playing and my father called it "pretty punk." Why? Why would he say that?

Now he apologizes, but it's too late. "I guess I just wanted the best for you," he says.

I can tell he really regrets not only that, but what seemed like a painful tradition regarding their only son. Vivian, a painter from the Rhode Island School of Design, who had won all sorts of fellowships, was very helpful to my mother, setting the table, moving the chairs around our living room/dining area, taking newspapers to the incinerator. The next morning, my mother whispered to me, "Do you really like her?" so I replayed the whole evening, trying to see what Vivian did wrong, even questioning my own affection.

And in college, there was Judy: short, a bit plump and always smiling. Her father was the chairman of the English Department and her mother an earthy person who loved to read. Judy took after her, and I saw myself following the footsteps of her father in all ways. We dated for a year, so my parents saw her often. For some reason, or maybe no reason at all, my father became convinced Judy's right leg was shorter than her left. He mentioned this again and again. She did have a little wiggle in her walk, which made him conclude that, if we married, our children would inherit her handicap. He used to get drunk and rave about it when we were alone.

He begged me to ask Judy to stand on one foot.

"I bet she can't do it!" he yelled.

"I bet she can!" I yelled back.

During one of our visits to Queens, in the middle of the usual lengthy cocktail hour, my father asked me to get the next round. I left him, my mother, and Judy in the living room, and mixed drinks in the kitchen. When I returned with the tray of Manhattans and Martinis, my father had changed the Peggy Lee tape, and he and Judy were holding hands and dancing to the "Hop-Scotch Polka."

Oh, you hop a little on your little left shoe
You hop a little on your right one too
You don't mind bouncin' like a kangaroo
To the Hop-Scotch Polka

He had gotten her to stand on one foot, and she was balancing herself, balancing crookedly, but balancing just fine nevertheless, and I was disgusted with him when I saw her inquisitive and trusting face smiling over at me.

MY FATHER'S RESPONSE

"Where I made a mistake," my father says, "was when I wanted to be good and helpful. You will make a mistake, like me."

"I hope not, not like that."

"Your mother and I wanted to guide you, that's all."

"I have to tell you, it bordered on abusive."

"That Anne would have done you in. You couldn't have kept up with her. In a few years, she would have stopped looking at you. Most wives are like that."

"What do you mean?"

"Your mother stopped looking at me. I remember around the time it happened. If I wore a new shirt or coat, she never noticed. She stopped listening too. She interrupted, noticing a sound in the air, or mentioning the heat or the cold. Really, without being seen or heard, you might as well be dead."

"You are," I say.

"But here I am," he says.

MILLIONS

At the foot of the Sagamore Bridge, there's an apartment building, a three-story brick structure that can be glimpsed from the highway. Closer to the road is its meager playground: a swing set and sandbox. Often a mother stands there, bundled against the cold, wearing a bloated ski jacket and knit hat, pushing her kids, similarly dressed, on swings. Mittens protect their hands from the icy chain links. Sometimes she is joined by another woman and her children. The traffic goes by, spilling exhaust their way.

Each time I drive past, I look over, and each time I ask myself: if I won the lottery today, $100 million, would I keep it, or would I rather see the winning ticket go to this mother and her children? Every time, I truly say: let her have it. Let her have the $100 million. I have said this for twenty-two years.

Today I'm changing my mind. Today I'm very close to keeping the money myself, but in the end, I don't. He gives it away, he lets her have it. He lets her have the millions that exist and don't exist.

DESPERATE? CALL THE SAMARITANS

It took just two years, 1933–35, to build this 275-foot-high bridge that crosses the Cape Cod Canal and connects the mainland to the Cape. And even more impressive: it crosses the river of forgetfulness and connects the mainland to the underworld. More memory is lost the farther you travel the sixty-two miles to Provincetown.

By the time you arrive at land's end, you have forgotten your name, your number, and how your day began. Before twelve-foot-high suicide barriers were installed, fifty-four people killed themselves by jumping. A suicide prevention group has placed signs that say *Desperate? Call the Samaritans* at the base of each side.

Sometimes an abandoned car alerts police to the possibility of a jumper, as did a woman's handbag found there in 1969. In 1984, a New Bedford man killed himself by squeezing through an opening in the bars where a tractor-trailer had crashed. In 1985, a fox, disoriented by construction, leapt to his death.

Last week, the bridge was closed in both directions when two of the Cape's most celebrated products met head-on. A pickup truck of tuna crashed into a trailer full of cranberries. The Bourne Police report noted, "Cranberries were observed covering the entire roadway."

The owner of the seafood company generously said he was not thinking about the recovery of its products.

"We're just worried about the health of our driver," he said. "While dead fish is our life, it's still just dead fish."

THE OTHER SIDE

On the other side of the bridge, I regain my memory and stop at McDonald's for more coffee while Anne waits in the car. I take a few sips and perk right up. On my way out, a man yells into his cell phone.

"It's Bill!

"Your son!

"Your son, Bill!"

The phone must have gone dead as he curses, stares at it, and presses buttons.

"Can you hear me? Mom?"

It's very much like the conversations I had with my mother during her final years. No matter what you say, when you say it twice at the top of your lungs, it sounds stupid.

My mother was capable of wordplay and punning right up to her death at ninety-five.

"Would you like another glass of wine?"

"Wine not?"

and

"They'll need a urine sample."

"Urine or my-ine?"

She never tired of mentioning the two greatest feats of man: flushing Long Island and wheeling West Virginia.

A few summers ago, I was at a dinner party in a secluded house in Truro and, before coffee was served, I went out on the deck to see the stars. A friend, Grace Hopkins, was there and said she was exhausted from her long drive to the Cape from Flushing, where she had picked up her mother. I told her I was born in Flushing. I mentioned my mother's pun about flushing and wheeling. She looked at me, astounded, and said that her mother, art critic April Kingsley, was from Flushing and her father, the painter Budd Hopkins, was from Wheeling.

TURN AROUND!

As I'm about to get into my car in the McDonald's lot, a boy yells, "Turn around!"

Did I drop something, forget something in my daydreaming?

No. He has a camera and is addressing the girl walking in front of him. She turns to face him and he shoots.

He was not the angel I thought he was, the one I wanted to obey, an angel ordering me home. He is a guy in love, capturing his girlfriend in a way she can't escape.

EXPECTATION AND ILLUSION

If you were stuck in traffic next to me and looked over, you'd see Expectation driving with Illusion, the inside of the car filled with the past that, like all of time, is indifferent in a week to a beautiful physique. Indifferent because of lost hope, not flagging desire. If I still had desires, I had no more illusions.

And you might see that as well: Desire driving, staring straight ahead, and Illusion sitting in the passenger seat, filing her nails.

HITCHHIKER

An old woman shivers by the side of the road next to the sign, *Driving Permitted in Breakdown Lane,* enduring the tumult of passing vehicles. She's clutching a black pocketbook by its long handles, trying to avoid the wind by bending her chin to her collar. I don't stop because I know that if I pick her up I will take her directly to her destination instead of dropping her off along the way, and risk being late.

She looks very much like my mother. I recognize the cloth coat, fake fur trim, and white brocade hat yellow with age. It could be the speed of the car and the plague of vitreous floaters blurring my eyes, but it does look like her, my mother, who died last year on Mother's Day.

"Don't pick her up," my father warns.

"I wanted to," I say.

"I know," he says. "That's dumb."

I've always given lifts to strangers, remembering *Love ye therefore the stranger for ye were strangers in Egypt.* But a few years ago, I found under my car seat a deadly but handsome blackjack, a sap, roughly eleven inches of flexible leather shaped like a shoehorn and filled with lead. Along the stitching, it gave the brand: Texas Longman.

A voice from the back seat says, "Did you think you could just leave me there?"

I see in the rearview mirror that it *is* my mother. She is laughing, happily shifting her shoulders and settling in. You'd think I'd be surprised, but why should I be? She can join me now as Anne, another ghost seen only by me, has joined me, as my father speaks, and as I speak to myself. Why shouldn't my mother come along on this final trip? We are all everywhere and nowhere and we are all together for the ride.

My Mother: Vices and Virtues

My mother's dominant personality forced me into situations that, even at a young age, I knew held peril. And yet in the end, I could not blame her because, after all, she had given me the gifts of intuition and insight that allowed me to foresee the fabrications, schemes, and mechanisms behind the visible world, the false gestures of strangers, the shortcomings of family members and friends. And yet, she was blind to occasions that caused me trouble. And yet, she was my mother, and I owed her my life. And yet, and yet … The relationship between mother and child is a long string of *and yets*.

At Beverly Farm, a resort in the Catskills where we vacationed when I was thirteen, we met a couple by the pool. The man, a creepy jokester doing card tricks, said he had an attaché case in his bungalow and he would show me the ways of *prestidigitation*. I didn't like the way he said the word. I didn't want to see those ways, and politely declined, but my mother insisted. On the walk over, he said, "Ever have your dick sucked?" and I left him there.

Marino's seafood market in Jackson Heights was a filthy, slimy place with fish placed on planks without ice, and turtles starving in baskets under display cases. Frank Marino asked if I'd like to eat a live sea urchin. My mother answered that I would love to and Frank reached beneath the counter and laid the black spiky thing on his hand, turned it over, cracking it with the tip of a rusty can opener, scooping out a plug of orange glop and telling me to open my mouth. It was delicious!

And yet.

John Skoyles

MY NAME IS JOHN

We pass a disabled bus, its passengers standing on the shoulder. The driver has opened a metal flap on the flank and is removing luggage. The logo says Casser Tours. I didn't know they were still in business.

When I was twelve, my mother accepted for me my Aunt Linda's invitation to go by bus with her to Williamsburg, Virginia, a five-night hotel stay, hosted by that company.

We left the Port Authority with an MC named Steve who told jokes and played games during the eight-hour trip in which the broken air conditioning stayed set on high. Everyone wrapped themselves in jackets and sweaters. There was no bathroom, so when we approached a rest stop, he'd ask, "*Oui?*" and if anyone answered, "*Oui! Oui!*" the driver pulled over.

Steve asked us to write a poem—it had to include our name and seat number. The winner would get a cigarette lighter. I was thrilled at this prospect.

A crusty old woman wrote:

> I sit in Seat Four
> My name is Augusta
> Turn off the air conditioning
> Before I bust ya

Mine was:

> My name is John
> I sit in Seat Three
> You know what I mean
> When I say *Oui! Oui!*

Steve read them aloud, and I was voted the winner. He called me up front to receive the prize. He held his closed fist high and then opened it, offering me a book of matches from the Howard Johnson's where we had just stopped.

124

I thought it was funny. I liked that kind of joke, but Linda was angry, sat straight up in her seat, clutched her purse, and looked out the window.

When we arrived in Williamsburg, the bus took us for a preview of the colonial village we would see the next day: the apothecary. Linda pushed me to the front of the demonstration where an actor in a lab coat and white wig opened a surgical kit containing amputation saws, arrow removers, a tonsil guillotine, and a circumcision knife. Then he displayed a jar of leeches and described bloodletting. The live leeches bounced back and forth in the water as he tilted it. I was already queasy, but when he placed the leech on his arm and it became engorged from sucking his blood, I had to leave. Linda took me to the porch where I sat on a bench next to a cigar-store Indian until my nausea passed.

Linda and I stayed in a single room. On the first night, thinking I was asleep, Linda hung her dress in the closet, took off her bra and panties, opened the dresser ... I couldn't take my eyes off her breasts and the brown bush between her legs. She removed a nightgown from the drawer and dropped it over her head. I was frozen with what, desire? I had had erections, but they rose and fell without ejaculation. I woke that night to my first wet dream.

We were exhausted at the end of the next day from the constant touring of museums and battlefields. Linda said she was going to bed early and put on her nightgown in the bathroom. I was in bed, my pillows propped up against the headboard and watching *The Life of Riley*. William Bendix kept saying to his coworker Gillis, "What a revoltin' development this is!" Linda sat next to me in order to better see the TV and asked if I was enjoying the tour. She said she was glad that the hotel had served pistachio ice cream, my favorite, for dessert and she mentioned the book of matches. I again said it was amusing, but I saw she had wanted the prize to be one of many highlights of this trip. She said, "Don't worry, I'll buy you a real cigarette lighter."

I started to get an erection, I couldn't help it. It happened all the time, even in church, coming back from the altar after receiving communion. The nuns told us to keep our hands clasped in prayer at our chests, but many boys had to cover their stiffening groins even as the body of Christ melted under their tongues.

I tried to reach for the blanket at the foot of the bed to cover myself, but Linda placed her hand under my pajamas. With a few strokes, I ejaculated, and she left for the bathroom, wiped me with tissue, turned the light off, and got into her bed.

I thought it would happen the next night, but she never mentioned it or touched me again.

When we got back to Queens, I met my friend Charlie who had returned from a week at Sag Harbor with his family. He and his father had just left the kennel where they had kept their German shepherd, Rico, during the vacation. Rico had always been calm, but now he jumped on the leash toward every passing dog. Charlie's father said that Rico had never been with a female before, that he must have had an experience at the kennel and would never be the same. I considered this as we parted and I ran up the stairs to our apartment's storeroom, the little unheated room in the hall away from the other rooms, and the only room in our railroad flat with its own door. I now preferred its seclusion, where fantasy and daydreams could bounce off its four walls privately, as they would for the rest of my life, as they do for everyone, all their lives; that's what walls are for.

MY PARENTS TOGETHER FOR THE FIRST TIME SINCE THEY DIED

The radio's traffic report alerts drivers to a detour in Cambridge due to construction.

"Remember the time I lost my legs?" my father asks.

"Yes, I do."

"That was pretty funny," he says.

He's referring to the time I took him and my mother to the Casablanca restaurant in Harvard Square. They liked drinking Jack Daniel's surrounded by the murals of Humphrey Bogart and Claude Rains as Sinatra sang on the jukebox. The Harvard poet, Jorie Graham, and her friend, sat at the next table. Jorie opened a black manuscript binder and began discussing poems.

When we got up to leave, my father couldn't move. He was more intoxicated than usual, perhaps from a mixture of medications, and my mother was tipsy. In other words, we were all drunk. My father put his palms on the table and failing to lift himself, yelled, "I lost my legs!" I moved between my table and Jorie's, apologizing for interrupting her, heaving my father up as he shook his head, smiled, and continued his refrain. My mother kept insisting to him that he hadn't lost his legs, that he should just put one foot in front of the other, and she illustrated this on the carpet, very nicely.

I got him to the Red Line and back to their condo at Charles River Park with my arm around his waist.

My father retrieved this as a good memory, but it was just a foreshadowing of what was to come.

CAMBRIDGE UP AHEAD

Justin Kaplan mimics the boasts of the kids in his son's Cambridge car pool. In the soprano voice of a schoolboy, he says: my father has an appointment at the United Nations; my father writes for the *New York Times;* my father won the Nobel Prize. I told him that a boy in our car pool was the son of the owner of I-CAN-DIG-IT BACKHOE SERVICE. Its brochure includes the testimonial: "Thanks for taking such good care of the septic. You were right, it was done with love and integrity," and the boy bragged that his father has demolished most of the old houses around town, and has fun doing it. Before he drives a backhoe through a wall, he paints the surface with a bull's-eye and then he and his men take turns aiming at it with a nail gun.

I took my son to Harvard Square and told him that he would notice a lot of men carrying purse-like bags over their shoulders and wearing berets. We stopped for a sandwich at the Blue Parrot. Customers hunched over leather notebooks with leather bookmarks that they had removed from leather satchels. They held their foreheads and looked into space, fountain pens poised over fountain-pen-friendly stationery. The café produces a literary journal, the *Perch,* and on the cover is a photograph of a man at a desk pensively resting his forehead on his palm and on the back a woman in the same pose. The next morning, Sunday, we went to a café called Mr. Bartley's for breakfast. As we approached the entrance, we saw a man in a beret, a satchel over his shoulder, standing there, reading a sign on the door that announced it was closed. He turned to us, made a face, and said, "*Quel* bummer!"

Final Exam

When my father died, my mother needed to go to a nursing home that accepted Medicare. She had suffered from severe dementia for almost twenty years and often confused me with her brother, my father, her father. The admitting doctor took her vital signs, put down his stethoscope and said, as she sat wide-eyed on the examining table, "She's in perfect physical health. It's too bad she's lost her mind." It was blunt of him, but not cruel. She smiled as he spoke, raising her eyebrows as if at a great compliment, understanding nothing, or maybe misunderstanding something, no foresight or hindsight.

She was in perfect health until she died the next day.

And now she is with me in the back seat. A ghost very different from and very much like the ghost next to me.

DOWN THERE

I tell Anne the story of the cranberry farmer, a former Provincetown resident, who lives with his wife and six children in this kettle hole off the highway, a hollow bordering the bog. The farmer confided to a group of us at the Old Colony Tap that he has never seen his wife undressed. She goes to bed wearing a white gown made from a sheet. When they make love, it is at night, in the dark, under the heavy fabric. This father of six said he wonders what she is really like "down there."

"I think a lot of men do, actually," Anne says.

I hope this isn't a criticism of me, so I ignore her and ask my mother, "Are you all right?"

"I don't know why I'm not in front," my mother says.

"It's safer," I say.

Anne says, "I hate that expression."

"What expression?" I ask.

"'Down there,'" Anne says.

"Why am I not in front?" my mother asks.

"You're better off down there," I say.

"Down where?"

"I mean *back there*," I say.

Anne takes a book from her bag of books, an anthology of contemporary world poetry. She leafs through it and says there is a new kind of poem being written in China. She reads, "It is a poem both present and absent. A poem seen in a dim light." She asks what I make of that.

"Where are we going?" my mother asks.

"To work," I answer.

"Probably abstract," I say to Anne.

"Where do I work?" my mother asks.

"I'm going to work, not you," I say.

"I bet you're right, those poems are abstract, that's what the translator must mean," Anne says.

"Can you find one?" I ask Anne.

"What I am going to do while you're at work?" my mother asks.

"You'll be with me," I say. "Don't worry."

"Don't lie to me," my mother says. She's getting irritated.

Anne says, "This is called 'Tents on a Mountaintop,'" and she reads it.

> A group of poets gathers on a mountain. There are rows of tents around them, and each belongs to a poet.
>
> Each poet has written a phrase or saying above the opening flap. I am told that I will have to come up with my own phrase if I want to live in one of the tents.
>
> I try to read the others' inscriptions, but they're written in a strange language, a code, or a foreign phrase.
>
> When I confide my lack of understanding to one of the other poets, he tells me that every phrase is meaningless, none of them make any sense at all.
>
> I feel better. And I feel worse. I will be able to join the group by inventing my own phrase, but I will be part of a fraud.

"You're lying to me," my mother says.

"I'm not lying to you," I tell my mother. "I would never lie to you."

"I like that," I say to Anne.

HER AGAIN?

This is the question my mother asks as she peers from the back seat toward me and reads my mind, something she has always seemed to do. "She's just a kid," she adds. "You have nothing in common." Anne has flipped the visor down and is applying eyeliner.

"She's not that much younger," I say.

"She'll distract you from the poetry you say you want to write."

"I've written more poems with her than with anyone, Mom. I wrote twenty poems the first month we were together."

"Maybe someday you'll write *one*."

Yes, Mom, she is five years my junior. Whether alcohol, humor, and a love of books constitutes common ground is the question. And the larger question is: when booze is involved, is that ground even valid? My mother doesn't ask that, and I didn't either at the time.

There's something lively in the union of humor and despair. Their offspring is dark wit. For Anne, now fifty-seven, the bleakly comic is still there: a vein of ore in a bedrock of privilege. Waiting to be mined, or never to be unearthed, who knows? I will try to bring it to the surface again, and bury this metaphor....

I recall our days together with happiness. She says it was a "dark time" for her, which disappoints me. Her memory shows I was part of a larger panorama, one figure among many. A boyfriend. There were girlfriends. Parents, one dying. Bosses, teachers, darkness pervading each of them, casting a shadow over those years, even when we held each other, the world to me, a netherworld to her.

"You'll be sorry," my mother says. "Mark my words."

"Mom," I answer, "you always said the most beautiful woman in the world was a blonde with brown eyes." Anne shuts the visor, her brown eyes sufficiently framed.

"You are *so* stupid," my mother says. "A blonde with *green* eyes is what I said! *Green eyes!*"

I have slowed to thirty mph without realizing it.

"Stop piddling," Anne says, "Step on it!"

132

I thank god my mother can't hear her, or she would say, "Piddling? What does that mean?"

"Brown eyes are a dime a dozen!" She adjusts her pocketbook in her lap, the righteous mother of a wordsmith.

Anne and I spent our evenings and weekends in Texas going from bar to bar. Chelsea Corners, The Knox Street Pub, The Jersey Lilly, Cardinal Puffs, Lyons' Pub, The Stoneleigh P, my favorite for the name itself: a former pharmacy, The Stoneleigh Pharmacy, its neon name in the front window with *harmacy* unlit.

I thought we'd get drunk again but instead we're sober together.

A Writer *Manqué*, a Son *Manqué*

"You should have gone to Paris," my father says. "That's what writers do."

"What made you think of that?"

"And I bet your mother would have agreed with me and named you differently."

"Why are you bringing this up?"

"Granville. Granville Skoyles. You would have done better, in Paris and with a name like that."

"It has a certain ring," I say, "but you got those names from a law firm. They weren't writers' names."

"They would have become a writer's name if you had one."

GRANVILLE

My father might have won
the war with my mother
and named me Granville,
a crowned head
on a brass plate
along the law-firm hall
he paced as a boy
delivering mail.
Runners-up were
Marsden and Coverdale,
heirs in plaid shorts
who waved from
Central Park's carousel,
then nudged their sailboats
farther and farther
from the sweltering shore.

A MUSE

Anne says she feels she has been a muse and nothing but a muse.

"Amusing," she says.

She says I only care about her as fantasy, not as a person, that she is more a phantom I invented to make a book that is very much like her: neither fact nor fiction. Or both fact and fiction.

"And yet you're alive," I say, "no matter what you call yourself. Real or imaginary. Actual or visionary. Memoir or novel."

"You have to choose," she says.

CLOUD

"I don't understand why we're in the car. Why don't we take a nice walk?" My mother hates driving, and never learned to drive, having grown up in a city where a vehicle was a nuisance.

I'm looking at myself as if from a cloud, as I did when her opinions separated me from myself and I had to act as if I were someone else. It's become a habit now, no, a way of life.

After she died, I felt her staring down from the heavens, judging me even from beyond the grave, and wearing the outfit she designed when most demented: her sweater pinned with two or three old Christmas cards, splayed open to show the sender's holiday message. But now she's in the back seat, shaking her head at the stream of cars and I wish I were going in the other direction, and staying for the rest of my life on the other side of Lethe, in the land of unconsciousness and the time of no time.

And yet I have to admit that even at home, I'm not at home. Bashō wrote:

> Even in Kyoto
> When I hear the cuckoo
> I long for Kyoto

And Quevedo:

> You will look in Rome for Rome, oh pilgrim,
> but you will not find Rome in Rome.
> What you are looking for is eternal and everlasting.

Two of You, Two of Me

I tune to a local radio station in Marshfield, telling Anne that local radio is best. Just then, the sports guy speaks so fast the scores run together incomprehensibly, and the weatherman drones on in a soporific litany of temperatures in nearby towns so that when he finishes we don't know the forecast. Ads for Natale's men's store mention Natale opening his first shop and placing his sewing machine in the window where he stitched and restitched the same sleeve to attract customers. Dockside Donuts on Sea Street makes its cinnamon buns sound so good, and I've always wanted to stop, but today is different, today is a day to live a little and Anne agrees, having fallen for the ad like me.

I'm driving slowly and Anne asks me why I'm going feather-foot on the gas. I don't want this day to end, I say, but maybe I'm not driving, maybe he is the one who parks where I've never been.

We take a table in the Dockside's patio surrounded by flowering forsythia and a birdbath with splashing chickadees. I'm surprised by the several sugar packets Anne cheerfully dumps into her coffee. Everything she does is cheerful, and her cheer is not vapid, the kind born of blindness to mortality and its path of ravages, not the cheer of optimistic naïveté, but a soulful goodwill. There is either a smile on her face or a fake pout that becomes a smile when she's granted a small wish, like stopping at the Dockside. I saw her alarmed only once, and she was grave for good reason—her mother was diagnosed with an incurable cancer. I mention this to her and she frowns for a moment, again calls it a rough patch, but looks over at me and says, "Otherwise…," drawing out the last syllable and letting it hang in the air followed by an ellipsis that I trace to its final dot, and where I hang inconclusively.…

She has brought a book from my attaché case, Auden's *The Orators*, which she flips open on the picnic table, and reads aloud a few lines: "One slips on a crag, is buried by guides, one is impotent from fear of judgment."

"And here's you," she says, "'one who believes himself to be two persons, is restrained by straps.'" She reminds me that I wrote her a letter once, as I wrote a letter to every student at the end of the term when I returned their portfolios. Two letters, actually: a formal letter and a personal letter. I thought this a profound demarcation. She thought it showed a divided self, a split personality, a forked soul. She answered me, the only one to do so—it was not required—with these opening sentences: "Now I get it. There are two of you."

One of us watches her pull down a branch of forsythia, bring it close to her face, and inhale. I do the same thing. I've reached the point in my life where I must enjoy every petal, every blossom, even when it has no fragrance.

A Writer *Manqué*, a Son *Manqué* II

"I'm proud of you, really," my father says. "I didn't mean you're not successful. I was trying to say I could have done more for you."

"You put me through college, Dad. Most of my friends had debts."

"You don't ski, golf, didn't go off to Paris. I should have helped. That's what makes bestsellers."

"Not really, Dad, that's a different world."

"I read the *Times,* I see what's going on. They make book deals on golf courses."

I held my father by the elbow to help him down the long hall in my house to the bathroom. As we walked, he looked through the tall windows facing the day lilies around the patio, and said, "You're lucky."

He meant it as a compliment, but I saw it as an appraisal of his own cramped and dim apartments.

It hurt the way my friend hurt when his mother, on her deathbed, guessed rightly that he was wearing a new tie.

My Mother: Virtues and Vices

When I was a little boy, walking home from the A&P with my mother, both of us carrying paper bags of groceries, we approached a mason who had just finished smoothing a new square of cement on the sidewalk with his spreader, and had roped off the area with a six-inch-high cord around its perimeter. He was on his knees, staring down at his job, and then he saw a bump or a mar, and he leaned over the cord, stretching above the surface and smoothing it out. He couldn't see my mother charging right up to him, raising her foot over the rope, as if about to place her shoe fully onto the fresh cement. She poised midair. The man looked up, shocked, in disbelief, and then he saw her smiling. And he gave out a great laugh. Relief, and some connection to my mother about the world of pedestrians, workers, pride in that work, worries about vandalism and a little bond between people who walk and those who literally pave their way.

Decades later, I took my mother to the Whitney Museum's opening of the retrospective of my friend, the abstract painter Myron Stout, who had given me tickets to the gala. My mother passed the white elliptical images on black backgrounds, the minimalist black ovals on white, looking, nodding, and drinking the proffered champagne. We were about to leave when I told my mother we should congratulate Myron. I found him surrounded by friends, collectors, and well-wishers, and introduced him to my mother. He said he hoped she had enjoyed the show.

"They look like the X-rays of teeth!" she said. "And toilet-bowl seats!"

Everyone turned away, except for Myron, who leaned toward her, touched her elbow, and said, "*My* mother thinks exactly the same thing."

And yet.

A Thank-You Note

As I mentioned, until recently I had had only one speeding ticket, for going twenty-five mph in a thirty zone in Fort Worth. Last week I was ticketed by the State Police for driving alone in the HOV lane. It's really an HOV trap as you enter Route 93 leaving downtown Boston, a half-mile ramp leading to the expressway. I've taken it for years, but a trooper pulled a long line of us to the side and gave out one-hundred-dollar tickets.

When he stood at my window he said it was an HOV lane and I said it wasn't.

With the practiced retort of a public official, he said, "Sir, there are seven signs saying HOV," and he poked his finger toward the skyline.

I said, "Haven't you read Neruda? Don't you know *We are many?*"

"Excuse me, sir."

I said, "Haven't you read Whitman? *I contain multitudes!*"

"Are you trying to be funny?"

I said, "Haven't you read Musil? *Our whole being is just a delirium of thousands.*"

He said, "Step out of the car, sir."

I said, "Can't you see there is someone next to each of us?"

The truth is I just took the ticket. This fantasy brings me to the fantasy girl once more. Anne was with me when I got that first citation. I should thank the vigilance of the Fort Worth Police Department. The ridiculousness of the offense made us laugh, and that was our first real night together.

INVECTIVE AGAINST BLONDES

"Are you married?" my mother asks.

"Yes, Mom, for a while now."

"It's about time, after all those floozies."

She begins naming them, counting them off on her fingers from that repository of memories that is still rich in certain synapses: Judy, Vivian, Lynne, Kathy, and the last one, the rich one, the blonde."

"She wasn't that rich."

"When you two showed up at the Alhambra, you had to keep borrowing money from your father. Or don't you remember?"

I'm amazed by this sharp recollection, but when it comes to her son, vitriol has always honed her mind and tongue.

My mother referred to our building at 37–15 Eighty-First Street by the name of the mural over the entrance, *The Alhambra,* a fake coat of arms the landlord painted in primary colors, hoping, perhaps, to live up to its namesake, a palace in Spain, and distract from the lobby, which was empty except for a five-foot-high machine in a corner that dispensed quarts of milk and chocolate milk. Water bugs jumped from crevices in the tile and flying roaches bounced off the walls. The landlord refused to replace the furniture after it was stolen a third time.

"*I* remember," my father says.

I say, "Yes, Mom, I remember very well."

I dread the memory. We came to New York to visit my parents over SMU's spring break. If Anne was shocked by my parents' tiny two-bedroom apartment in Jackson Heights, she didn't show it. More likely, I paid no attention to her response. I paid attention to little in those days. One morning, I overheard Anne telling my mother in the kitchen that she had to take me shopping because I hadn't noticed that no one was wearing bell-bottoms anymore. My mother said that I was not a slave of fashion, and added something about my being a slave of women.

I did have to keep asking my father for cash. And I remember him smiling amusedly as he opened his wallet and peeled off his last twenty with a father's goodwill, saying, "She is not a cheap date." He was right about that.

"Yes, she had expensive tastes," he says.

"I appreciated the money, Dad, but please don't butt in. I'm trying to tell a story."

"Whatever you say, John."

Anne had made a list of places she read about in *Cue* magazine. She rented roller skates in Central Park where she circled round and round. I watched her pass as I sat on a rock. A restaurant called The Sign of the Dove, a place for engagement celebrations and marriage proposals. She pointed out how beautifully the skylights illuminated the Venetian glass figures. A glass of wine cost three dollars. In Queens, a dollar and a quarter was top shelf. Maxwell's Plum, a singles bar frequented by celebrities. Roy Eldridge played at Jimmy Ryan's. I found an inexpensive dinner at Reidy's, which embarrassed me because a banner above the menu said *It's Not Fancy, but It's Good.* I told my mother about this loud slogan when we returned to The Alhambra and she winced sympathetically. At the Museum of Modern Art, I was glad Anne had her student ID for the discount and I recall our joking with the clerk at the admission counter that she had all A's and I had given her one of those A's and the cashier said he bet it was for effort.

Anne's father and brother joined her in New York, to spend the weekend celebrating her brother's birthday and then take her home. Her father, a kind man, had a doctorate in literature as well as his law degree. Her brother, an aspiring actor, worked at a high-end men's clothing store in Dallas and had just finished performing a major part in *The Knight of the Burning Pestle.* He wanted to see as many plays as possible and to sample fine cuisine, but he complained that in Texas he gauged the quality of a restaurant by the number of luxury cars outside, a template useless in New York.

So Anne left The Alhambra to stay at the Four Seasons with her father and brother. On their last night, they kindly treated me to *Sweeny Todd,* and then to dinner at "21." Over Irish coffee, Mr. Fletcher gave his son a birthday gift, a Rolex Submariner wristwatch. It was a beautiful thing, which I praised as I held its stunning heft, but their heads turned when I read the name on the face aloud, as the "sub-ma-*reen*er."

Anne told them she wanted to have a drink with me alone. She grabbed my hand and brought me to her hotel room where she pulled me on top of her. I was so excited by the clandestine moment and luxuriant furnishings, that I came prematurely, and withdrew for fear of making her pregnant. I apologized. She said, "I thought you would have brought something," meaning a condom.

I received a letter from her the next week saying she missed me, but also noting that I had worn brown shoes with a black belt and that the lapels of my sport coat showed that it was long out of date. And the hotel bar, where we drank, is known as The Re-*al*-o, and not, as I had called it, "The *Real*-o."

She hurt my feelings then and she was riding beside me now, in that world I have never left, where the real and the Realo meet and each imbues the other....

THE HOSTESS WITH THE MOSTESS

My phone rings. It's Mary Stair. She owns a Truro mansion with views of the ocean, the bay, and Pilgrim Lake. I don't want to go, I don't want to accept her invitation, I try to refuse, but each time I tell her we are busy she suggests the next night, and the next, and the next.... There is no winning. I will have to go to Mary Stair's for dinner.

I have been there before. She sits at the head of the table and makes requests, saying, "Tell the one about how you had to pick up bets for your uncle in Manhattan." I had to retrieve this information for the command performance, acting it out, straining, as it did not come naturally. Others were called upon to recite their set pieces. After each, Mary bowed her head, expressing delight at the story, her good taste in dinner guests, and her role as emcee.

She greets each guest at the door, graciously, saying, "So glad you could make it," and giving two kisses.

The odd thing is that now, at functions of any kind, public or private, no matter where, whenever Mary sees me, she says the same thing, "So glad you could make it," as if she were the hostess. She has done this at fund-raisers for a museum, a gallery opening, and a poetry reading. And she even did it at a memorial service for a close friend of mine, for whom I was giving the eulogy. "So glad you could make it," she said as I arrived at the door of the meeting house. Whatever the occasion or location, once her guest, always her guest.

REPLY ALL

I check e-mail on my phone. The director of undergraduate admissions is asking us to make the titles of our courses "sexier." He singles out "Literary Foundations," in which Homer, Virgil, Ovid, Sophocles, and Plato are discussed, as particularly boring.

I write, "How about 'Last Tango in Athens'?" and hit Reply All, something he would have done, but now I did it.

REAL LIFE

"What's that music?" my mother asks about the CD I'm playing.

"It's Nino Rota," I tell her, "the guy who does the music for Fellini."

"Oh," she says, having forgotten Fellini and the time I took her to *Juliet of the Spirits* at the Jackson Theatre in Queens.

She had become curious about Fellini when I was in college because he was mentioned in *Il Progresso,* the Italian newspaper. I had to convince her to go because the Catholic Church's Legion of Decency rated it Condemned. I told her they were probably prejudiced against Italians, something she believed, having experienced it herself. (She insisted she was denied a job as a typist because she was given a trick test that said to copy a page, including the phrase NO CAPS ALLOWED, which she typed verbatim, only to be told she failed because no capital letters were allowed. She said her Irish girlfriend was given a different exam.)

At the point in the film when Juliet overhears her husband on the phone making a date with another woman, my mother leaned over and said excitedly, "Oh, this is when she kills him!"

"No," I whispered, "foreign films are like real life. She'll just be unhappy."

My mother was quiet for a while, watching Juliet sulk. Then she said, "If you want real life, why go to the movies?"

My Dream

I tell Anne about the dreams I've been having, and she says she records hers in a journal she keeps in her bag. She suggests we exchange dreams and I tell her my most recent:

The receptionist, Denise, at the front desk at Emerson calls to say a bald man was there and asked, "Did you attend John Skoyles's funeral?"

I say this sounds threatening and Denise agrees. She says the man just left and I might be able to catch him.

I'm rushing, but I have to take a piss and stop by the men's room. When I leave, I'm limping. I've left one shoe by the side of the urinal so I run back to get it.

On my way down the hall, I see I've now lost the other shoe. I go back, but each time I leave the men's room, I'm missing a shoe.

I give up and stare at my face in the bathroom mirror, and it is the pale and vacant face of a corpse.

GENESIS AND EXODUS

Eddie Harris plays saxophone on "Theme from Exodus," a top-forty hit from my childhood. Every time I hear it, I think of morning in our apartment on Judge Street, my mother loading laundry into the washer between the sink and the stove. There's the smell of Tide and toast. The radio is tuned to WABC, with Herb Oscar Anderson saying, "Good morning, Mama! You're looking great today!"

My mother lived to the theme from Exodus and died in a nursing home called Genesis.

"I died in the hospital's Epoch wing," my father says. "Where do they get these names?"

Of Today

A colleague calls to say Emerson is holding a party to mark the end of a capital campaign at the Kowloon Restaurant in Saugus, which serves Chinese food and seats twelve hundred.

"I bet it's not as good as the Dragon Seed," my father says. "But let's try it."

"Not today," I tell him, but I don't say never.

When I was a kid, I went with my father to pick up food from the Dragon Seed, the Chinese restaurant in our neighborhood he preferred to others, saying it was "more Chinese-tasting." He always greeted the men at the Dragon Seed bar, which seated only four. He told me that the biggest drunks were those who hung out at the bars of Chinese restaurants. I enjoyed his theories, but they drove my mother crazy. He appeared gentlemanly because he bought smart suits, but he was really of the streets and wise to their ways. Once, sitting in our Mercury Comet on the Shelter Island ferry, we were approached by a man going car to car, holding a can of some kind and talking to the drivers, a captive audience. When he reached us, he said to my father, "Know what I'm doing?"

"I'd say you're selling," my father replied. It took the peddler aback, and he moved on with his can of instant flat-tire repair.

He used to tell me to think of sailboats when I couldn't sleep as a child, but I had never seen a sailboat. *What is a sailboat?* I asked. He said *It's a boat with a long pole sticking up from it and attached to the pole are sheets that fill with wind that blow it across the ocean.* He said to think of sleep as the time when streets are rivers with sailboats on them. This kept me awake even more.

In his retirement, my father progressed from doodling to painting. After all, it was in his background; his father painted. He took a class at PS 145 and produced landscapes he gave to friends, except for one he was fond of: children wading in a lake, huddled around a toy sailboat. I was going through an existentialist phase in college when I came into the living room and saw my father staring at his painting.

151

I said, "I think you should have put one of these kids facing another direction, toward the horizon." My father considered this, and said, "That would be more of today." A funny but familiar phrase, *of today*. He put my remark in context: I was looking through the eyes *of today*, a cultural and temporal pinprick.

I wish he had been happier at the end, at the Mayflower Place Retirement Community. Because he scrimped and saved, he could afford it, but it placed him and my mother among members of the upper crust. He mentioned that whatever table they sat at for dinner in the dining room, they were with graduates of prep schools and Ivy League colleges. Their dinner companions once asked my mother for her favorite classical composers and she couldn't name one. My father said they continued to press her, saying she must have a favorite. Mozart? Bach? Brahms? Finally, my mother said she was not interested in classical music. They asked what music she enjoyed. She replied confidently, "Semiclassical." My father saw their sneers, but paid them back a few minutes later when two men at the table said they were members of Mensa. They asked my mother if she was familiar with that organization. My father answered, explaining to her that it was a club that was very hard to join, because members had to have a high IQ and be stupid at the same time.

His favorite sound was a good laugh and he had one then.

ANNE'S DREAM

Anne opens her journal and reads:

I am watching my dead mother from above, as if I'm on a cloud, looking down at her in the house I grew up in. She is trying to call me on her old-fashioned rotary phone, but it's disconnected. She picks up an alarm clock and turns its hands around and around, as if dialing. The phone rings in my purse! It must be my mother! She has somehow been able to call out on her alarm clock and I am thrilled to be able to speak with her. I reach in to answer and find, not my phone, but the old kitchen timer she used to keep on the stove.

No One Knows It, but ...

I used to stop at Jimmy D's in Quincy for two quick Martinis on my way home from school. I was truly an anonymous alcoholic here, a total stranger, giddy with my first drink after a day of teaching and the start of the long drive. Men at the bar knew each other well and spoke in familiar, comforting refrains:

What're you gonna do?
Don't blame yourself.
It's surprising who'll disappoint you.
She probably didn't mean it.
I'm not expressing it exactly right.
You don't have to tell me.
It probably wouldn't have lasted.
I thought I could count on him.
You can't change people.

One evening the phone rang constantly, and each time Jimmy answered, he didn't wait for the caller to speak, but said brusquely, "We're not showing the fight tonight," and hung up. He explained that the callers were not interested patrons, but the "Pay Per View Police" who wanted to catch bars showing a championship boxing match to a crowd for the price of a single viewer.

The man next to me described his hobby: tropical fish. He had just bought a pair of blind cave fish for his aquarium. He said they will bump into the coral, the bridge, and other objects along the bottom, but only once, then they learn the way. He kept repeating, "They learn through experience, they learn the way," with great satisfaction, when all the TV screens lit up and the fight came on.

CIRCUS SCHOOL

"The exit for the zoo is here, Mom. The Franklin Park Zoo. Nothing like New York, but I hear it's pretty good."

"I don't like zoos," she says, "not after that monkey hit me in the eye with a sweet potato."

"That was the Bronx. They're not like that in Boston."

"Don't treat me like one of your students. Can you turn down the heat?"

"I'll put on the air."

"If you like it this warm, why don't you move to Florida?"

"I don't think my wife would go for that."

"Are you still with her, the fat one?"

"What are you saying? She's not fat!"

"Yes, she is, you met her at the school for clowns. I remember!"

"No, I didn't."

"Yes, you did. That's what you said. You met her in clown school."

"You're thinking of the joke I told you years ago: *I met my wife in circus school. I was studying to be a clown and flunking out. She was studying to be a fat lady and getting all A's.* Does that sound familiar?"

"To each his own."

155

THE FACTS

The general practitioner sent me to a urologist in Hingham. My wife accompanied me because it is said that at medical visits you need a second pair of eyes and ears, someone to listen clearly and get the facts straight without emotion.

The doctor said, "You have a fairly enlarged prostate."

All the way home we debated what he meant by *fairly*.

MY PRICE

Anne says, "My father said that if I was serious about you, he would put you through law school. I never told you that."

"That was generous," I say. "How come you never mentioned it?"

"I didn't want to put any pressure on you."

"And you didn't know if you were serious about me."

"We were serious," she says, avoiding the issue.

My father says, "Is that your price?"

"Not that again," I say to him.

This is what my father said when I was in second grade and came home with an assortment of school supplies. I told my parents that Sister Mary Helene left the classroom and put me in charge. She ordered complete silence and told me to write on the blackboard the names of those who talked, which I did. One boy said he would give me a pen if I erased his name. Soon I had a whole array of stubby pencils, ballpoint pens, and rulers. And no names on the board.

My father took a look at the loot, all of which I was very proud and very covetous. "Is that your price?" he asked then as he asks now.

I tell my father I would have turned down the offer.

"You might have done better taking it," he says. "Especially with her tastes."

Anne adds, "And he said when you got out, you could join his law firm."

"The price is higher now," my father says.

"The price is higher now," I tell her.

"What price?" she says. "I remember in those days you were thinking of following in your father's footsteps."

She's referring to the end of my appointment at SMU as visiting professor, with no job in sight, when my father called to ask if I wanted to take over his accounts at the Connecticut Valley Paper & Envelope company as a salesman. He said it was easy, I would simply renew his customer's orders every year and spend the rest of the time writing poetry.

I told him I'd think about it. I didn't want to hurt his feelings by immediately spurning the offer. As soon as I got off the phone with him, I went out drinking with Anne.

When I was drunk, I told her that maybe I should take the job because when it comes down to it, everything, really, is an envelope. I held up my Martini and said, "What is this glass but an envelope for your drink? And the bar, an envelope for drinkers. We sleep in an envelope called bed."

"It's funny that you became the lawyer," I say.

"You know, I almost forgot I was a lawyer," she says. "This whole trip, I've kind of forgotten who I am."

"I know. On this trip, you are mostly who you were."

"If we had stayed together, I wonder what I might have become," she says.

"You should see what you look like when you say that."

"When I say what?"

"If we had stayed together."

"What did I look like?" she asks.

"I thought for a minute you were getting a Monster Face."

HELEN KELLER'S BATHING SUIT

"I don't know. Honestly, I don't know," said Michelle Cook, the director of the Wrentham library, about how the rare-book room came to possess the deaf-blind activist's black linen two-piece composed of a long, flowy sleeveless top and bloomers, plus a pair of knee-high stockings.

This article from the *Quincy Patriot Ledger* reports that it was donated at some point to the Wrentham Historical Society and stored at the library. The society has since disbanded, raising the question of whether the library is really the owner.

Cook said the swimsuit was photographed, digitized, and entered into an online, searchable database. "And the cool thing," she added, "is that you can see it there for free."

EVIDENCE

The exit to I-90. When I was a kid, my parents moved from New York to Granby. My father commuted more than ninety miles to his job at Logan as an airplane mechanic. He couldn't afford anything closer. My memory is of metal walls because we lived in a Quonset hut in a park of Quonset huts. I played with the kids next door, the Kwasnik family, five girls, each with a runny nose which they wiped on their sleeves. I did the same, infuriating my mother. I tried to stop, but it had become a habit. One day I came home, cold as usual, to the cold house. She asked me if I had wiped my nose on the sleeve of my sweater. I couldn't remember, I thought not, I hoped not, I said no. She pulled my left forearm in front of me and slapped the back of my head. I remember one thing very, very distinctly: I associated this moment as "evidence"—something kids talked about playing cops and robbers, and now it had convicted me.

I was often sick, and my mother took me to the doctor, who said to keep the house warmer. My mother replied that the other kids played in the same weather, slept in the same cold houses, and seemed fine. The doctor said, "They're used to it. Those families have been living like that for generations." This gave my mother an air of superiority, as if my fragility proved we were better than the Kwasniks.

Several weeks after we moved in, my parents invited the Kwasniks for drinks. When my father finished taking their requests, I asked, "May I have a cocktail?" The girls gasped and their parents were shocked.

My mother said, "Oh, we don't give him a cocktail, just some grenadine and club soda."

"No," one of the girls said. "It's not that. We didn't know he could talk!"

My mother told me this story, more amused than alarmed. She said I would often run into the house asking for cookies or chips, which she gave me to distribute. It seems that although I spoke freely at home, I returned to the girls and never said anything at all.

The medical practice calls it Selective Mutism. The Creative Writing Department calls it Memoir Writing, and I teach it.

Out on My Feet

I'm less struck now by the not-speaking part than I am by the content of my request, which followed me until I was sixty-two, when I thought I had shadow-boxed with alcohol for more than forty years only to discover it was real boxing, and I had been knocked out but was still standing.

TONY'S PUSHCART

My mother likes the Jimmy Durante song that comes on, "Did you ever get the feeling that you wanted to go, then you had the feeling that you wanted to stay."

"I have a whole CD of him, Mom," I say.

"Oh, that's great," she says. "Does it have 'Tony's Pushcart?'"

"I don't think so," I say. "I don't remember that one."

"You'd know it if you heard it."

"How does it go?" I ask.

"It doesn't go, you have to push it!"

A MANILA ENVELOPE

Anne pulls a brown envelope from her large handbag and shows it to me. I ask what's in it and she says I'll see. Eventually, she says. I say please, but she smiles that crooked smile and puts it back into her bag. We pass a prep school where the teachers' union is about to call a strike and a huge hand-painted white banner flies over the roof: *In Hoc Fer Plenti,* fake Latin to satirize the poor handling of finances by the administration.

I tell her I took Latin and recommended it to my son because my two years had served me well. Unfortunately, at Nauset High, Harry watched films like *Ben-Hur* and *A Funny Thing Happened on the Way to the Forum.* He came home humiliated one day because he was paired with a poor student in an exercise that required reading aloud each other's translation of "The Three Little Pigs" to the whole class. Harry had to recite a mistranslated sentence that he knew would bring ridicule and hilarity.

He read, "I'll build my house of brick, *said the pork.*" And chaotic laughter followed.

Anne asks if all of the students were that bad. I tell her that one day a substitute history teacher asked the class what would have happened if England had won the war with the colonies. A boy's hand shot up, the teacher called on him, and he guessed, "We'd all be speaking English?"

The teacher flew into a rage, and said, "You are the dumbest, most stupid boy! We *are* speaking English!" Further answers of the same sort provoked more incredulity and fury from the substitute.

Harry said that just before last period he saw the teacher being escorted from campus by two policemen.

Was there anything good in the school, Anne asks.

Yes, the school orchestra where my son learned to play guitar. Then I recalled another story. Harry said that during a rehearsal, the teacher/conductor lost his temper with a violinist, a new student who had transferred from Juilliard, and reprimanded him for playing faster than the others. Yet the boy continued exhibiting his up-tempo style. Enraged, the conductor threw his baton at the boy, stormed off the podium, and headed for the exit. As he reached the door, the new boy yelled, "Fuck you, Maestro!" The teacher/conductor shouted back, "It's too late to apologize," and left.

"Now can you show me what's in the envelope?"

She just smiles and turns and looks out the window.

"It's too late to apologize," she says.

CAPTIVE

All art is made in order to seduce, to capture an audience, sometimes an audience of one. Sometimes it works, sometimes not. If the latter, the beloved remains a fantasy.

Kafka asked: *Could it be that one can take a girl captive by writing?*

Years ago Anne and I stayed in the Amherst Motel, and drove around the hills of western Massachusetts in the evenings, chasing sunsets and drinking beer. We parked near Bare Mountain, spread a blanket on the overlook, enjoying the dusk. When the sky darkened, we packed up and drove slowly downhill. A woman walking the same way signaled us to stop, leaned into the driver's side window and said, "You have a spaghetti pot on the roof of your car." I had chilled the bottles in that big aluminum tub I borrowed from the motel and filled with ice. Leaving the bluff and having drunk all the beer, I had forgotten about it.

I feel a little drunk now and, just like then, it's going to get dark soon, and my prisoner could escape.

THE WILD IRIS

I often listen to audio CDs on this drive, among them, Allen Grossman's lecture, "Poetry: A Basic Practice," Seamus Heaney's lavish brogue, and Louise Glück's reading at the Academy of American Poets. They pass the time, yes, but I find myself going slower and slower as I get more and more absorbed, often imitating their idiosyncrasies of speech for amusement, particularly that of Louise because the students refer to her "poet voice," a tone incantatory, lilting and light years away from common speech.

Even now-ow the hil-ills are assembling-ing ...

My friend Burkard calls, the speakerphone interrupting the recitation. He asks what I'm doing and I tell him I'm driving to work with the ghost of my mother and listening to a Louise Glück reading.

"Your mother must love that," he says.

I look over my shoulder. "I think she's asleep," I say.

"Your imitation will wake her up," he says.

"Not today."

"Come on!" he says. "I need a laugh."

"Sorry." I begin to laugh myself.

"Come on, do Louise Glück! I'd love to hear it. Do Louise!"

My mother is awake. She says, "What's going on?"

"Do it! If not for me, then for your mother."

"For my mother? What are you thinking? First I'd have to tell my mother who she is."

My mother catches my eye in the rearview mirror, leans forward, and says, "Who am I?"

THE PORPOISE AND THE FRENCH FRY

An ad for the New England Aquarium comes on the radio. When I went with my son, we were greeted at the door by a hundred penguins. A giant fiberglass ocean tank built around an artificial coral reef stood in the center, housing sharks and eels and enormous turtles. They do not attack or eat each other because they are meticulously overfed. A touch tank allowed us to pet sting rays.

On our way out, we joined a crowd standing at the base of an above-ground glass tank watching a porpoise. He poked his nose into the bottom corner, trying to reach a long french fry (crinkle-cut), but the force of his arrival caused it to rise to the surface. Then it slowly drifted down. He lunged again, and again it rose. The crowd followed its trajectory, all heads moving up, then all the way down, where the poor thing once more charged the corner. The potato went up and down, the creature went back and forth, our heads rose and fell....

If it weren't for that french fry, the whole place would have seemed unreal.

TRUE STORY

After my reading at the Marshfield library, the host, who was a poet, gave a reception at his house. Every end table held a white marmalade jar of sharpened pencils and a stack of index cards. Everyone at the party was a poet, every poet was the publisher of his own press, and every publisher, the editor of the magazine it produced. One of them called it a local neurosis.

There was another local neurosis. I met three people with variations of the same verbal tic. One said, "*Okay?*" after every other sentence, asking if you had understood. For example, "When we got there, the cops were waiting for us. They had been tipped off. Okay?" The other did not ask, but just made his point by using the word *point*. As in: "When we got there, the cops were waiting for us. Point: they had been tipped off." The other ended each anecdote with the label: *True story!* He said, "When we got there, the cops were waiting for us. They had been tipped off. True story!"

Point: each had his own verbal tic, okay? True story!

John Skoyles

CLOSE UP

"Are we there yet?" my mother asks.

The traffic is bad and we're hardly moving.

"No, not yet. It'll pick up soon. Look out the window," I say.

"There's nothing to see."

"Look at the trees. Some buds are starting."

"Trash," she says.

"You can see the woods," I say. "When I take the bus and this happens, I look at the ground close up. You see all kinds of stuff."

"I don't like things close up. Everything close up is ugly. You should know that."

ENTRE NOUS

My friend Tom never reveals a thing about himself, but when we drive, like we did the other day to visit Johnson's Tree Farm in Falmouth, he speaks openly. Facing straight ahead does that to him; he goes on and on: Tom almost became a surveyor. He never liked his wife's body. He collects Post-it Notes from work and hopes someday to make a collage. He's bought a tub of Mod Podge to do it. His real name is Ptolemy.

I understand. Maybe this is why psychiatrists ask their patients not to face them.

And now you understand why I have created another self. So I can talk privately to you on this trip, not facing you and behind a shield of glass.

Remember ...

Anne asks me to stop at the Burger King at Exit 14 so she can use the restroom. I get out to stretch near my car, which I've parked in the shade by a dumpster. One of the BK workers on his break comes over and stands next to me, lighting a cigarette. He's in his seventies, tattooed with images from another age, a wreath above an inscription of which I can read only *Remember* ... He asks about the Venza, then says, "I'm looking for a new car myself. I went to the Ford dealer on the weekend, and a salesman comes up wearing a hat, a derby or something. He says, 'I'm Cap.' He says I'll remember his name because he always wears a hat. I thought that was pretty good." I agree. And then he says, "Cap asks me, 'Thinking about buying a car?' I say, 'No, I'm gonna buy a car. I'm thinking about pussy!' That really got him! Didn't buy a car, though."

Anne walks out and stops in the sunlight, takes a hairbrush from her purse, and brushes each side of her head, back and forth, back and forth.

The worker looks at her and says, "We won't see that again."

I say, "Things are not what they appear to be."

"She's with you?"

"Yes and no."

"I get it," he says. "She represents your yearning to live. She's a figure for male egoism, which loves not so much the woman but its own fantasies about the woman, and sacrifices the actual person to the literary phantom, so as to give birth to a work of art."

I walk over and open the door for her.

"That's it, more or less," I say.

THE END AT THE MAYFLOWER

We hid my mother's dementia to gain access to the Mayflower, but it came to haunt us.

My parents moved in with no trouble and moved out with nothing but trouble. My father fell in the bathroom of their atrium apartment, the place where, when it was first shown to them, the director said, "A wonderful woman lived here whom everyone loved."

My mother said, "Oh, that's nice. Where'd she go?"

The director was openmouthed, but my father answered, "There's only one place you go when you leave here."

And he went there.

When he fell, he broke his pelvis and lay in the kitchen, asking my mother to call the front desk. As soon as she left the room, she forgot about him, returned later, and asked him what he was doing on the floor. He told her to dial the phone or open the door and get help, which she said she would do, but again she forgot. When my parents didn't appear at dinner, someone went to their apartment, but by that time hours had passed, sepsis had set in, and he was taken to Cape Cod Hospital in critical condition.

PHONOPHOBIA

The dean calls just as I approach Boston and wants to know if I've made up my mind about accepting his offer to be associate dean. We had a talk last week about the post, and when I found out it paid nothing except release time from teaching, I declined. I'd rather teach. Still, he asked me to take a day or two to be certain. I thank him once more, but I'm not interested.

I tell Anne. I want her to be impressed. And I have made an impression, but from an earlier time at SMU, when I taught a poem by Cavafy that she remembers.

"It's like the great yes or the great no," she says.

I know the poem by heart:

> For some people the day comes
> when they have to say the great Yes
> or the great No. It's clear at once who has the Yes
> ready within him, and says it,
>
> he goes on to find honor and respect.
> He who refuses never repents. Asked again,
> he'd still say no. Yet that no—the right answer—
> defeats him the rest of his life.

"Is that good or bad?" I ask her.

"It's both," she says. "And neither."

"Very helpful," I say.

"You were polite on the phone," she says. "There's a smidgen of *yes* still in you."

"I know," I say. "I felt it."

I didn't like the phone call. Not because of anything the dean said, but because I could hear my voice. I could hear what I sounded like to him, like I was listening to a recording of myself. As if there's a division between body and soul and, as they have their discourse, I'm eavesdropping on myself, as if he is listening to me learning to say no.

THE HOUSE OF THE RISING SUN

Anne asks to drive and I ask if she is crazy, since she's never been on this busy highway and doesn't know the way. She just stares at me, her bottom lip in that fake pout. My father used to say, "If you're going to do something, do it graciously." So she takes the wheel at the next rest stop.

"The House of the Rising Sun" plays on Pandora's Hits from the Sixties. I bought that single as soon as I heard it when I was fifteen, mystified by the lyrics but understanding something like pain in the voice. I took it to my friend Herbie's house and played it for him and a few others. They hated it. Herbie screeched, "Whatever possessed you to buy that record?" I recognized his mother's scolding tone which he was now applying to me. It only made me love the record more and isolate me further from the boys on my block. At home, my mother helped me figure out the lyrics, and explained what "on a drunk" meant. She was always open to music, poetry, art, anything she saw as something she should know and wanted me to know. When she died a year ago, on Mother's Day, I didn't miss her, so now why did I put her in the back seat, why am I crying?

OLD SPICE

Anne looks over, merges right, and says, "You smell like my father," with an expression that in the best light might be called a fond, nostalgic glance. When I was in college, I wore Old Spice aftershave. It was what my father used and his father before him. Girls would say, in a trusting tone, "You smell like my father." It was a passport to intimacy.

Forty years later, the scent has remained the same.

"Get the envelope," she says. "In my bag."

"My father told me when I was a kid never to look into a woman's purse."

"Go ahead," she says, swerving by a pothole.

I find the envelope and unclasp the fastener.

"It's your letters to me, your love letters," she says.

"Oh, no," I say, sifting them out.

"My dog chewed some. A funny thing happened. My husband, he's the jealous type, so when we got married, he wanted me to destroy them, but I hid them in the attic. We moved and I forgot them. A year later, the woman who bought the house called and said she had something of mine, and I picked them up."

"I don't know if I want to read them," I say.

"It will show you who you were back then."

"I guess I'm curious," I say.

"And who I was," she adds.

I page through and read some passages.

> *June 11*
> Your letter didn't come today. Probably tomorrow. I miss you
> in a way new to me: I find myself conversing with you and
> writing long letters in my head. Needless to say how much I miss
> making love and sleeping with you. Just writing this is getting me
> depressed ...

June 12
After I mailed my letter to you yesterday I walked back from the post office and thought I hadn't said what I wanted. You are a joy to me, alone and in company.

August 6
I miss you and love you very much, you must know that. I went to a Chinese restaurant and my fortune said, "The answer lies within." Or does it *lay* within?

August 24
No matter how long a letter I write, it doesn't seem to say anything I feel. Thanks for the crushed flower.

September 10
This time last year I was trying to figure out how to ask you to go for drinks.

October 10
If I sound a little abstracted or bland, please forgive me. I have a head cold and a cough and can't think straight. I need my vitamin back, the blonde one.

October 24
It was October 27 last year that we first went out ... I'm making use of your absence to remember you.

November 5
Any time you want to visit will be fine with me. I'm living on very little money but will save up so we can go to good places in Boston and here too. I will take you everywhere in P'town.

December 22

I didn't mean to make you feel bad about going to Spain. I was shocked, though, that you're staying so long.

THEN AND NOW

after Galeano

Opening his e-mail, a man read a brief note from a former girlfriend of many years ago.

They corresponded, and she sent him a list of books she loved. When he turned the pages of one of them, he felt he was beside her on a couch, and they were reading it together, as they used to do.

She sent him a photograph of herself standing next to one of her watercolors, her hair tied at the back of her neck. The painting was the same blue color as her dress.

He couldn't take his eyes off of her leaning against the gallery wall.

She looked back at him, held out her hand and, who knows how, carried him away.

She placed him behind the wheel of a car, and they drove forever in what seemed like one long day.

At nightfall, she returned to the gallery, and he went on without her.

So brief was that eternity that no one noticed his absence. And neither had he noticed that his girlfriend's hair in the photograph now flowed loosely over her shoulders.

WHEREVER YOU'RE GOING, I'M GOING YOUR WAY

We slow down next to an electrical crew fixing power lines. My mother points to a worker and says, "I remember that man, the one in the red sweatshirt."

This is similar to her saying, as we passed Quincy, where she had never been, "I remember this place."

Statements trying to show that she has not lost her memory but proving she had.

Twenty years of dementia, twenty years of not being anywhere in the world but somewhere in the past where she was happiest snapping her fingers, dramatically rolling her eyes, and singing:

> Oh Thunderwurst, oh Thunderwurst, how could you was so mean—
> for having invented the sausage meat machine?
> Now all the rats and dogs and cats are never to be seen.
> Oh Thunderwurst, oh Thunderwurst, how could you was so mean?

and:

> They called her frivolous Sal
> A peculiar sort of a gal
> With a heart that was mellow
> An all-round good fellow, was my old pal
> Your troubles, sorrow and care
> She was always willing to share
> A wild sort of devil, but dead on the level
> Was My Gal Sal.

Now she sings a few bars of a very mournful "Moon River," *Two drifters off to see the world ...* which changes into Mantovani's "If I Loved You," the semiclassical version.

DRINK

I love the stretch of highway from which you can peer over and see Milton. There's the Toy Chest, Salty's Diner, and a bar with no name but a one-word neon sign in the window: *Drink*. Drink. A year after my father died, I was feeling a little blue, and one evening, having a few Martinis, I said to my son, when he asked what was wrong, I said it had been a weird year, with this problem and that issue, and "dumping my father into the drink."

Startled, he stared at my glass of gin in horror, and asked, "Into what drink?"

My father, even from the afterlife, continues to alarm his male offspring.

I point out *Drink* to Anne.

"That's as close to a drink as we'll have together," she says.

"Maybe there's another kind of oblivion," I say.

"You're there now," she says.

THE DEATH OF MY FATHER

He told me from his hospital bed how my mother kept forgetting he was on the floor and kept forgetting he couldn't get off the floor. He said, "She kept repeating, 'What are you doing there? Get up! Get up!' and walked away."

His body rejected the antibiotics that would knock out the infection. Each day when I visited, he was weaker and could no longer sit in a chair. He had to be propped up in bed.

A nurse said, "He's your dad? This guy has issues!" She said this right in front of him, just as the doctor had said about my mother that she was out of her mind. At first I was offended for him, but then I realized he couldn't hear her, or I hoped he couldn't.

I turned his bed toward the window, a view of the parking lot, but better than the wall. That was the last time I saw him.

I left the hospital and headed for my car but, before I got in, I realized there was a slight chance he'd be watching. I paused and turned toward the building. He was on the third floor. I guessed which window might be his, and I waved. I felt stupid waving at a building, and it had started to snow very lightly, almost beautifully, the lights on the roof catching the steady flakes. I waved again and, from many windows, pale hands waved back, hands of the sick and dying, hands that belonged to those who thought they might have recognized me, or maybe the hand of one who did.

"I did see you," my father says. "And I waved back. Good-bye again, John."

Aces High

The sky darkens; it looks like rain, and yet I feel a little lift of spirit, as always, passing the hundred-and-fifty-foot water tower which Sister Corita painted with loud splashes of color, a rainbow swash brightening Dorchester. Dorchester! How often I went drinking with my friend Emilia on its streets. She favored a bar called Aces High, and in Aces High, it's bottled Bud and a big handwritten inscription on the wall that said *Girls Rule*. I'd invite her along, but the car's already filled with too many memories.

Objects, people, the landscape, none of it seems real through this windshield, which, as I drive and dream, becomes more like the electronic screen of a labyrinthine game, a maze of delights, obstacles, and detours. Each pedestrian a target, each driver a piece on a road map, a maze like Chutes and Ladders.

I have always kept my distance, stayed in the middle lane, as a good motorist should, maybe guided by the wrong driving instructor, who taught that only as aesthetic phenomena are existence and the world really justified. Then again, maybe *The Birth of Tragedy* was an inappropriate driver's manual.

We savor these long spring days, yet today is different, shorter due to an odd impending darkness. The day seems a fantasy until I take Exit 20 toward the stark realism of Chinatown and South Station. I got in the car as a young man and am driving now recalling him with a memory that prides itself on remembering instead of simply doing so. And in a robotic way, I cannot tell the past from the present, or this place from another, but I know that the people are real, at least as real as I am. I see myself again from above, one of many who are either maturing or aging, dying or about to be born—the latter two on their separate ways to hospitals, each in an ambulance, one heading south, the other north. We pull to the side and let them by.

THE LAST LOVE LETTER

Anne is deftly weaving in and out of traffic. She's wearing sunglasses even though it's getting dark and she tightens her grip on the wheel in that way that reminds me of the beauty in her strength.

"There's one more letter," she says. "I put it in the glove box."

I remove it. It seems no different from the rest. She says, "It's the last one."

> *February 29*
>
> I never received a letter from you in Dallas, though I did receive a card with a fishnet on it.
>
> You are right when you say my last letter to you was ice-cold. I wasn't at all angry that you were going to Spain. I did feel shabbily treated during those weeks, however. When you told me that you were staying in Europe for a few more months after school ended, and that your father and brother were joining you, I couldn't help feeling the fool: here I was in P'town, hoping to see you over Christmas, and if not then, at least in the spring when you returned. Then I found out all at once that neither was possible. If I saw you in July, that would be an entire year. I guess I haven't felt included in any of your plans, and that's what accounts for my cold tone.
>
> I can't get angry at you, as you asked in your letter. I just feel we aren't such important parts of each other's lives. In your card you said you were fatalistic enough to believe that if something were meant to be maintained between us, it would. I don't see things that way. It takes work; things don't just happen. I couldn't help but feel you weren't trying very hard to see me.
>
> I think of you often and of our times together. When I got your card and you mentioned Austin, my heart sank. I kept it on the end table and it depressed me each time I looked at it. I don't have any bad feelings toward you at all. I just know that to continue this wouldn't be good for me, and I'm sorry.

Each day I wear the beautiful scarf you sent me for Christmas. I love it. It's replaced my brown one.

Maybe it's just that you're more independent than I am and can pick things up again. I worry and doubt too much and know what causes me pain. Perhaps I'm not strong enough for you.

I am seeing a woman here, a painter, and getting along well. I hope you will write to me and stay in touch. In writing this letter I don't know when I've been too honest and then maybe not honest enough. I feel everything I've written here and it's been very hard to say.

I want you to know that I feel a lot for you and our time together. I haven't distorted it the way you feared I would.

Please write.

I fold the letter and slide it back into the envelope. I have an odd memory. Twice in Dallas we were approached by photographers. The first was a warm fall day, on the bank of Turtle Creek where we were lying on the grass. A reporter from the *Dallas Morning News* walked over, aimed his camera, and said he had a gotten a great shot. Our response was both shy and slightly boastful—we didn't want to be seen together publicly, and yet we enjoyed the humming thrill of the small scandal in our relationship. We asked him not to use it. The other time we came out of my apartment in the morning to a blizzard. I had an ice scraper, rare in Texas, and was chipping away at the windshield when a TV news truck approached. The cameraman filmed me hacking and Anne waiting, but again we declined. Two records of our time together, there and not there.

I'm staring at the letter. Anne is waiting for my reaction. The letter is an obvious attempt at self-preservation. I don't know whether to apologize, or to make light of it. I see my chance for levity; I had used a semicolon. The letter drew me back into my days of living on the fellowship stipend of $150 a month, paying eighty for rent. If I had had the means, might I have flown down to see her? I was once surprised when she showed me a credit card, something beyond me. Why was I so passive, why didn't I literally go for broke?

I turn to tell her this but when I do I'm looking only at an empty seat. I see straight through the driver-side window to the cars passing on the left. The past was driving, the past that was very much past redeeming, and now it has gone back to where it belonged, leaving me here, a passenger alone in a moving car.

FREEDOM UNDER LAW

In sixth grade, I came home from school, very excited, and told my mother we were taking a class trip to the Statue of Liberty. She was ironing in the kitchen, the room filled with a dreamscape of steam that I found both stifling and pleasant. She didn't look up.

"Did you hear me, Mom? We're going to the Statue of Liberty!"

"You forgot to put out the garbage cans and we missed the truck," she said. "They'll stink for a week."

I apologized and said I would roll the cans into the basement.

"They should take you to the Statue of Responsibility," she said.

I'm taking responsibility now. I've crawled into the driver's seat, remembering Paul Resika's advice to his lovelorn student that in every relationship there's a driver and a passenger.

Still, I've left behind liberty and freedom. No, I'm driving in a country where there is freedom under law, where each imbues the other....

THE DEPARTMENT

The retreat will begin at two o'clock in Room 528 of the Walker Building on Boylston Street. As I get closer to campus, I visualize walking down that hallway among my colleagues, especially my soul-mates: Jonathan-Soup-With-Fork, whose lively translations of Jacques Prevert feature dreaming donkeys and art supplies; Melina, the passionate Greek, whose laughter makes trivia disappear; Trimbur, the Old-Marxist-Young-at-Heart.

Most of the others were happiest in graduate school when they were the smartest students in class. Now they are herded into a department with the rest of the smartest. Their years of study were in color; the remainder's black and white.

The door to Dr. Robertson's office is always open as he counsels students to write not, "I think that...," but, "Therefore, permit me to posit ..." A young critic, sunglasses perched atop his head, gesticulates wildly at the copier about his new article he is pinning to the bulletin board, saying to no one and everyone, "Queequeg is the book! Queequeg *is* the book!" The mild new hire, a woman from Purdue, is happy to be in Boston. I told the chair I liked her, but he said it will be a while before we know if the egg will produce a serpent or a dove. The professor of electronic publishing does everything virtually and yet here he is, mournfully keeping required office hours none of his students attend. The lone teacher of studio art has an office among us, no one knows why. A gruff, wild-eyed Austrian, he stands behind his desk, waving a brush and saying to three terrified students, "In the left hand, the magic of chance! In the right, an engendering urge!" It's said that the habit of analysis has a tendency to wear away the feelings, and the winner of the Pulitzer Prize for criticism, a magnificent essayist, is relentlessly incisive in person. She described the reading of a young poet as like listening to someone recite an unfinished crossword puzzle. At lunch with her one day, she had the hostess move our table three times: chilly from a vent; noise from the kitchen; too dark in the corner. She asked me to read the draft of a love letter to the man she hopes to persuade to leave Berkeley and join her. I wanted to say that passionate words shouldn't be written in drafts, but I told her it was fine, though I did insist she remove the semicolons.

Members of the Developmental Promotion and Tenure Committee can be heard in the conference room debating whether tenure should depend on publications in "venues of reputable authority," or "venues of national reputation." The debate is winding down in favor of "national" when the Greek notes her work appears "internationally," and the argument begins again, rises and falls and is finally tabled until next month.

The Undergraduate Curriculum Committee fights over approving a workshop devoted to flash fiction. A writer of historical novels pounds the table, saying that teaching the short-short is like training students to address an envelope when we should be instructing them to write letters. The flash fiction teacher says, "Don't disparage my course!" The historical novelist scoffs and says, "*My* course! *My* course! Those who say *my* course are like the breeze that passes through a tree and says *My* tree!"

Everyone avoids Professor Opanstopi, who had to undergo mediation with many students for his harshly written critiques of their work. I recall his scathing assessment of my advisee, Anna La Fredo: "When the heroine of a LaFredo essay has a toothache, the world must moan."

The Continuing Education Task Force, of which I'm a member, meets every week from two to four. Last week, the chair said we were ahead of schedule, so we could hold the next session from two to three. The acting chair of the Acting Department objected, saying, "Why don't we stick with the two-to-four slot, because it feels so good when you get out early."

My office is on the hall with the other writers, poets, and playwrights, broken animals longing for the infinite.

The Moments

The department chair calls, says the secretary is home with a sick child, and asks if I would mind taking the minutes. I say I'd be glad to, but I hate taking the minutes. No one reads them except the chin-scratchers who point out the misspelled name of the person who seconded a motion; that there were two abstentions, not three ...

It will be hard for me today, because today I have replaced appointment with chance, schedule with happenstance, minutes with moments, each moment a cradle and a casket.

Today I'm living where moment and memory meet, the syllable and the sound, the greeting and the goodbye....

The minute hand stands still, then it jumps, and in between, there is the moment.

POPCORN MIX

I had forgotten how it ended and see in that last letter that I removed myself from Anne, as I could read all the signs up to that point.

After that, I patched myself up, filled in whatever was missing like a crater in a street, filled it with boiling tar and gravel poured into a hole worn in the asphalt like those ruts on my block in Queens. The laborers were always Italian, and my mother always sent me out to them with a jug of cold water. One man leaning on a shovel saw me looking at the pitch and pebbles and explained in broken English that it was a "popcorn mix." This gave it a snappy, party-time feeling, and it served the street for a while, but soon it opened again, that abyss, and the men returned.

THE GREEN LINE

Passing Arlington and Boylston's T stop, I remember taking the Green Line at Longwood Medical Station, near Northeastern University. The trolley is coming and so too is a crowd of students, talking and laughing and horsing around. Among them is a beautiful girl, a child really, maybe eighteen years old. She talks with the others and I stare at her profile, hidden by the long brown hair she keeps tossing from her face. We all board the car, and she gets on, or does she? I turn in my seat, this way and that, as if I have lost something or someone. She has taken the boy I was and shown him to me, a boy watching Hayley Mills in *Tiger Bay* when I was ten and had a crush on her, and she reminds me of Anne, another tomboy, another testosterone-laden female. I check myself to be sure that glimpsing the girl was not made of desire for more than the past. When a woman kisses an ugly thing in "The Frog Prince," she is rewarded by his transformation into beauty and wealth. Now I understand the other side, the frog becomes a boy with a full head of hair and strong arms, and not a tattered thing upon a stick, leaving the urologist with a prescription for Flo-max, the sheath having outworn the sword. The frog longs for the girl, knows his desire is impossible, and accepts his fate. A kiss changes an old man to a boy, the boy to a prince; maybe such a thing can happen and I have missed my stop.

LOSING MY MOTHER (AGAIN)

When my mother became senile, I lost her in the present, when I was with her, and had to keep reminding her of where she was, and who I was. And then I lost my mother as she was in the past, all those good years when she tended me as a child, took pains to ease my pain, taught me large things like respecting the work of even the lowliest laborers. As well as small things: in a restaurant a gentleman always checks his coat, hoping I'd be a gentleman. Those years blurred and erased by years of her introducing me as her brother, her husband, her *who*, she'd ask me, *are you?*

She's looking around the Venza. "When did we get this car?"

Her mind is focusing a little better; the ride has stirred something. She's now aware of her surroundings, but with a distorted context and wrong frame of reference. She strains forward, between the front seats, and asks if I love her. "Of course," I say, "Why do you ask?"

"Because," she says, "sometimes you are mean to me."

I have never been mean to her. I understand from her questions that perhaps my father has been mean to her, and she is stroking the back of my neck, tenderly, as if trying to recover herself through her relationship to my father, but she has the wrong man.

She begins to cry; not cry really, but sniffle. She goes through her purse to find a tissue, digging to the bottom of that bag she left behind in so many restaurants in her fading years. I adjust the rearview mirror and see her unearthing packets of sugar and saltines, along with a transparent plastic rain bonnet folded into a triangle.

I skip over decades of dementia to recall her funny comments, like when my wife, exasperated by my mother's constant punning, said, "I must have done something awful to get a mother-in-law like you!" To which my mother replied, "This is your *pun*ishment!" And to a waiter who came to our table with a tray of bourbon on the rocks and one glass of water, which he spilled slightly: "He can hold his liquor, but he can't hold his water."

I was out of town the morning she died. I had a new cell phone which malfunctioned taking voice mail. I came home that night to a message on my landline from hospice saying they had been trying to reach me, that she had had a massive heart attack.

"Where are we going?" she asks again.

"I'm going to work."

"Then where am I going?"

"You're going with me."

She starts to hum "Moon River," and looks out the window, already having forgotten her question.

The traffic has stopped, bumper to bumper.

"Where did you say we were going?"

"To school, where I work."

"I remember that man!" she says, pointing to a state trooper in sunglasses standing near a work crew at Exit 17.

"That's good," I say.

My mother undoes her seat belt, leans forward, and reaches around my head, trying to cover my eyes. "Guess who?" she says.

I ask her to please stop, to stay in her seat.

"Guess?" she says, climbing toward me.

"It's my mother," I say.

"No!" she says. "Guess again."

"Olga Bertolotti."

"Guess again!"

"Mrs. Skoyles."

"No!"

"Please!" The traffic is picking up and I have to merge right to get off. She is reaching around the side of my face.

"Guess who?" she repeats. "Guess who?"

"Mom!" I say, losing patience.

"Right!" she says.

And with that, my mother goes back to her grave, because that is what graves are for.

THE FUTURE, THE PRESENT, THE CONDITIONAL

The retreat will begin.
The retreat begins.
The retreat would have begun.

It's Not Fair

It doesn't seem fair to be living again the pain of that final letter to Anne.

When I looked into her eyes, I was swirled into a nautilus, a shell, the divine proportion of the logarithmic spiral. Heady and romantic words, I know, but surrounding those heavily perfumed phrases was a normal world where she walked her cocker spaniel, Bitty Lou; mixed perfectly pale margaritas; poked fun at my semicolons, and breathily answered the phone at the restaurant where she was hostess: *Sleepy Hollow,* four syllables in which I wanted to lie down for twenty years.

She traced her heritage to the *Mayflower,* a descendent of John Fletcher, while my family arrived on the *Niña,* the *Pinta,* or the *Santa Maria,* mangling vowels. Did opposites attract, or was there friction and flame from the start?

I wish he had that fireboat.

THERE AND NOT THERE

I have never been good at recognizing the difference between what's there and not there, discerning truth from the invisible truth. My days with Anne included infertile eggs, a printed book never published, wedding rings joining no one together, undeveloped film, and a phantom child.

When I was a little boy, my aunt took me to Central Park to ride the carousel and visit the zoo, which abutted a small cafeteria where you could have lunch. It was very crowded, but we found an empty table and my aunt told me to wait while she went inside for sandwiches. A woman approached holding a bowl of soup. She asked if anyone was sitting there. I couldn't believe she could ask such a stupid question—it was obvious no one else was sitting at the table, and I told her so. She sat down, removed the lid from her soup, and began to eat. A few minutes later, my aunt returned with a tray, totally shocked when she saw the woman. The woman said she had asked me if I was alone and I said yes. She gave me a horrible look and got up. My aunt gave me a horrible look and sat down.

I told my mother this story when I got home and she said I was the stupid one. A few days later, we went to the A&P on a busy Saturday. There were no shopping carts, so when a woman checked out, my mother grabbed hers, and gave it to me to push. She placed a loaf of Wonder Bread in the cart and went to the vegetable section while I waited. A man with his arms full of groceries approached and asked if that was my only item. Again, I was struck by his blindness, stupidity, I didn't know what to call it. I told him yes, that was all I had in the cart. So he dumped his stuff right next to the bread. My mother returned, and she yelled at me for being an idiot and at the man for taking advantage of an idiot.

I stand by my statement that that was all I had in my cart. And that there was no one beside me at that Central Park table. I will insist on these facts again and again, the same way I believe that those who were with me today are with me now.

John Skoyles

In a nightmare I am playing strip poker with Anne and we are both down to underwear. It's my deal and the cards are covered in maple syrup, and my hands, the chips, the table, everything is sticky from the excessive, spilled sweetness. I win, and she stands, puts her thumbs inside her underpants' elastic band. I'm looking at her face, which has an impish smile, and at her panties which she lowers little by little by little until she pulls the cloth down quickly, and between her legs is an infinity sign.

Infinity Again

Love is not infinite, but it's infinite while it lasts.

Arrival On The Common

The retreat is supposed to begin at two o'clock in Room 528 of the Walker Building on Boylston Street. The sky is heavy, like a fruit that ripens and ripens but does not fall to the ground. A flock of geese, ten or so, flies unusually low over the traffic, approaches my car from the rear and then, startlingly, hovers next to my side mirrors as we cruise down Arlington Street close to Boston Garden and its pond where the Swan Boats glide. A honking goose almost hits my car, then lands, or tries to, in the empty lane on my right, making a harsh belly-flop. I see the cause of its error: oil puddles on the dark asphalt which the lead goose has mistaken for water. It lifts off and goes its way seemingly unhurt, victim of a mirage.

The line of customers outside the stone kiosk on Boston Common housing The Earl of Sandwich shows the charming evolution of city life. The lunchtime franchise used to be a men's room in the 1920s. As the *Boston Globe* put it, "formerly a locked tomb encasing ancient urinals and rusting pipes."

Dogs romp across the small green pasture, chasing balls and Frisbees. Children picking flowers from the perfectly geometrical beds leave gaps that give landscaping the look of life. An ancient Asian woman practices Tai Chi and reaches her toe toward the sky. The streets are laid out with New England common sense: Arlington, Berkeley, Clarendon … Common sense. The last time I heard the phrase was when my father died. A priest from the hospital called, saying that since he had lived until ninety, it was time for him to go because, "For the most part, God uses common sense."

In this last decade, I've begun to wince involuntarily at the lack of common sense of strangers, even those in the news who have danced off rooftops, stolen petty cash from thrift shops and purses from coworkers, driven drunkenly on the rims of their tires until they ran out of road. A weakening of my mind, or softening of the heart? Perhaps just grieving over the plight man was born for, and myself I mourn for.…

The corpse is the perfect fusion of the person you were and the person you wanted to be, the priest told our grammar school class on a field trip to the funeral home. By dividing myself into me and him, I felt free, yet each in the cell of himself is convinced of his freedom.

When I left the house today, I knew today would be different. It is very different for the crushed squirrel on the down ramp to the parking garage, his tail quivering in the breeze from passing cars; for him, it was like any other day, only shorter. When life stops, death also stops, someone said in an attempt at consolation.

My passengers have left, the car is empty and yet I can't help look around. I had two parents and lost them both. I loved one woman and lost her twice. The Hancock building's beacon glows a steady red for rain ahead, and the office windows are lighted against their concrete frames. It's midday, but night is arriving, a pall across the city. The life we didn't lead, that's our real life. Saint Augustine warned us not to step outside ourselves; the coach advised us to stay within ourselves. Maybe this was bad advice. Dusk overtakes the city and shadows merge with those who cast them. The streetlights come on only when darkness falls; that's their real life, and now they are making shadows of us all.

A stop sign gives me a chance to look into the park where a female cardinal lands on a litter basket. The female cardinal is my canary's favorite. When I place Godzilla's cage near the kitchen window overlooking the birdfeeder, I watch him sing twice as hard when she arrives on the perch. She turns to the sound but hears only a few notes, his song muffled by the glass where she sees her reflection, leaving Godzilla like the writer who describes an old flame and in doing so paints a picture that does not remind her of him, but of herself.

One must wait until evening to see how splendid the day has been, and I cannot complain, although I wish I had not dwelled so long in the literature of despair, the stories and facts that disrupt simple happiness. Beethoven's Hammerklavier sonata arrives with a little static from Cape Classical, 107.5, which is coincidentally my odometer's exact reading at this moment, the mileage from Truro to Boston. In the house in Vienna where Beethoven died, a young philosopher shot himself in the heart. Why do I remember both deaths equally? Because the young man had described so vividly his bewilderment on looking back on the road just traveled, at the indifferent street that showed the irreversibility of time and he reasoned that his backward glance showed the nothingness of it all.

I drive into the underground parking garage on Charles Street and my car disappears from sight. As I make a right turn, I see the arm of the entrance gate is raised. I can go right through without paying! Without taking a ticket, just as the cars ahead of me have done! I follow them, happy to be free of the exorbitant charge, and this small thing renews my hope that yes, today is different. As I follow the ramp to the middle level it occurs to me that I have forgotten something, and that is how I will get out, but there must be a way.

I park and open the door onto the garage floor where an array of lottery tickets, newspaper pages, and a square of delicate pink tissue paper flutter past. A wise man told me to live in the layers, not in the litter, but maybe there was something to be salvaged there. Salvage was the name of my favorite shop to explore as a boy when my father drove us on a Saturday afternoon to Freeport on Long Island.

The retreat begins at two o'clock in Room 528 of the Walker Building on Boylston Street. My colleagues, seated at long tables or gathered at urns of coffee and hot water, will be expecting me. Or maybe they have given up waiting, and the chair will ask someone else to take the minutes. The minutes. The name alone deadens the heart.

And this is how it gets to be too late, slowly and permanently too late.

I am permanently late now, and everything is dark.

Notes

Some sentences and phrases have been taken from the following writers and poets:

Adolfo Bioy Casares: The people are real, as least as real as I am.

W. H. Auden: Time that is intolerant / Of the brave and the innocent, / And indifferent in a week / To a beautiful physique.

W. H. Auden: And each in the cell of himself is almost convinced of his freedom.

Cesare Pavese: If I still had desires, I had no more illusions.

Primo Levi: Their years of study were in color; the remainder's black and white.

Enrique Vila-Matas: Every hope is an egg that may produce a serpent or a dove.

Henri Michaux: Man is a hobbled animal longing for the infinite.

Claudio Magris: In the same house (where Beethoven died) on the night of October 3rd–4th, 1903, Otto Weininger shot himself through the heart. A few weeks earlier he had described the feeling of bewilderment one feels upon looking back upon the road one has just walked, the indifferent street with its rectilinear length that speaks of the irreversibility of time. In the end, this is all there is, the backward glance that perceives the nothingness of it all.

Claudio Magris: She had been the symbolic figure for male egoism, which loves not so much the woman but its own fantasies about the woman, and sacrifices the actual person to the literary phantom, so as to give birth to the work of art.

Philip Larkin: Excerpt from "Days."

Ruth Wallis: Excerpt from "Senorita What's Her Name."

Robert Musil: Our whole being is just a delirium of many.

Johann Wolfgang von Goethe: Looked at from the height of reason, life seems like a grave disease, and the world like a madhouse.

John Skoyles

Dawn Powell: There is only one city for everyone just as there is only one major love.

Friedrich Nietzsche: Only as aesthetic phenomena are existence and the world really justified.

Eduardo Galeano: Love is not infinite, but it's infinite while it lasts.

Toon Tellegen: This is how it gets to be too late, / slowly and permanently too late.

Robert Walser: I had risen up, to go home, for it was late now and everything was dark.

Alan Dugan: Possessed of an echo, but not a fate.

Acknowledgments

Portions of this book have appeared in slightly different form in *Brevity*, the *New York Times*, the *New Yorker*, and *Plume 7: New Poems 2018*, ed. Daniel Lawless, and *Woven Tale Press* VII:2.

"Granville" previously appeared in *Inside Job* (Carnegie-Mellon University Press, 2016).

About the Author

John Skoyles' most recent books are *The Nut File; Inside Job;* and *Suddenly It's Evening: Selected Poems.* His work has appeared in the *New Yorker,* the *New York Times,* and *The Atlantic,* among others. He is the poetry editor of *Ploughshares.*

www.ingramcontent.com/pod-product-compliance
Lightning Source LLC
Chambersburg PA
CBHW030318020726
47493CB00004B/1074